YOU 'WILL' WIN

WIN

The One Stopping You Is 'You'

By:

Alden Crestwood

Acknowledgements

Writing this book has been a journey of reflection, perseverance, and learning. It would not have been possible without the support, encouragement, and inspiration of many individuals.

First and foremost, I am deeply grateful to my family, whose unwavering belief in me has been my greatest source of strength. Your love and encouragement have fueled my determination to bring this book to life.

To my friends and mentors—thank you for your invaluable guidance, wisdom, and honest feedback. Your insights have helped shape the direction of this book, making it more meaningful and impactful.

I also extend my heartfelt appreciation to everyone who has shared their stories, challenges, and triumphs with me. Your experiences have provided invaluable lessons and motivation that are woven throughout these pages.

A special thank you to my readers—you are the true reason for this book. May these words inspire and empower you to break through barriers, believe in yourself, and achieve the success you are capable of. Remember, **YOU 'WILL' WIN—The One Stopping You is 'You'**.

Alden Crestwood

Table of Contents

Section 3: Taking Action

Section 4: Creating Your Path to Success

Section 1:
Understanding the Barriers

Chapter 1: The Invisible Chains – What's Holding You Back?

You are meant to win. But if you aren't winning yet, it's not because of an external force stopping you—it's because of invisible chains holding you back. These chains are not physical, but they are just as real. They exist in your mind, in your habits, and in the stories, you tell yourself every day.

What Are These Invisible Chains?

Imagine an elephant tied to a small rope. When it was young, it tried to break free, but the rope was strong enough to hold it. Over time, the elephant stopped trying, believing that escape was impossible. Now, even as a powerful adult, it stays tied—because it no longer questions the rope's strength.

You, too, have invisible chains—limiting beliefs, self-doubt, past failures, fears, and negative influences—that keep you from moving forward. The biggest difference? Unlike the elephant, you have the power to break free.

Identifying Your Chains

Before you can break these chains, you must recognize them. Here are some of the most common barriers that hold people back:

1. **Fear of Failure** – The belief that failing is the end rather than a stepping stone.

2. **Self-Doubt** – The inner voice telling you that you are not good enough.

3. **Procrastination** – The habit of postponing action, waiting for the "right time" that never comes.

4. **Perfectionism** – The unrealistic need to get everything right, which leads to inaction.

5. **The Comfort Zone** – The safety of routine that stops you from growing.

6. **Negative Influences** – Surrounding yourself with people who reinforce self-doubt rather than push you forward.

7. **Comparison** – Looking at others and feeling like you're behind rather than focusing on your own path.

Do any of these sound familiar? Chances are, you're carrying more than one of these invisible chains.

The Story You Tell Yourself

What you believe about yourself shapes your reality. If you tell yourself, *"I'm not good at this,"* or *"Success is for other people,"* then your mind will find ways to make that belief true. The problem is not ability—it's the story you keep repeating in your head.

But what if you changed the narrative? Instead of *"I'm not good at this,"* say *"I'm still learning, and I can improve."* Instead of *"Success is for other people,"* say *"Success is possible for me if I put in the work."*

Consider this: Have you ever heard someone say, *"I can never remember names"*? They repeat this statement so often that their brain accepts it as fact, and they make no effort to improve. But memory experts prove that name recall is a skill anyone can develop with practice. The difference? The story we tell ourselves.

Your brain is wired to look for proof of what you already believe. If you believe you're not good at something, you will notice every failure and ignore every success. But if you believe improvement is possible, you will start looking for ways to grow.

Breaking Free Starts with Awareness

Most people go through life unaware of these chains, convinced that external circumstances are stopping them. But the truth is, the greatest obstacles are within.

Here's your first challenge:

- Take a notebook and write down at least **five things** you believe are stopping you from winning.

- Now, for each one, ask yourself: *Is this really true, or is it just a belief I've accepted?*

- Next, rewrite these statements into something empowering.

For   example:
✗ *"I can't start a business because I don't have experience."*
✓ *"Many successful entrepreneurs started with no experience—I can learn along the way."*

Your mind will resist this exercise at first. It's comfortable with old beliefs, even if they limit you. But if you commit to challenging them, you'll start breaking free.

The Science Behind Mental Chains

The reason these invisible chains feel so strong is because of the way our brains are wired. The human brain prioritizes safety over growth. This is a survival mechanism from our ancestors, who needed to avoid risks to stay alive. Back then, stepping into the unknown could mean death. Today, stepping out of our comfort zone might mean facing failure, rejection, or uncertainty—but not life-threatening danger.

Your brain doesn't differentiate between real danger and perceived danger. That's why public speaking, starting a business, or making a big life change can feel terrifying—even when logically, you know it won't kill you. The same neural pathways that helped ancient humans survive now keep you stuck in patterns of self-doubt and hesitation.

But here's the good news: The brain is changeable. **Neuroplasticity** proves that our thoughts, habits, and beliefs can be rewired. When you consistently challenge limiting beliefs and replace them with empowering ones, your brain adapts. Over time, you form new mental pathways that lead to confidence, action, and success.

This is not just self-help talk—it's neuroscience. The more you practice a new belief, the stronger the neural connections become. Think of it like a hiking trail. The more you walk a path, the clearer and easier it becomes to follow. If you stop walking an old path (self-doubt) and start using a new one (self-belief), your brain will eventually default to the empowering thought.

A Personal Story: Breaking My Own Chains

I once met a man named Dave, who had spent years believing he wasn't meant for success. Growing up in a small town, he constantly heard statements like, *"People like us don't achieve big things,"* and *"Success is only for the lucky ones."* These beliefs became his invisible chains.

For years, Arjun played it safe. He never applied for better jobs, never took risks, and always doubted his abilities. One day, after attending a seminar on mindset, he realized that he had been living with someone else's limiting beliefs. He asked himself, *"What if I just try? What if I stop assuming I'll fail and see what happens?"*

That simple shift in thinking changed his life. He applied for a better job, started networking with successful people, and eventually launched his own business. Today, he runs a successful company, and when asked what changed, he says, *"I stopped believing the lies I had told myself."*

Your story may be different, but the lesson remains the same. The only thing stopping you is the belief that something is stopping you.

The Truth: The Lock and the Key Are Both in Your Hands

The biggest realization in your journey to winning is this: **You are both the prisoner and the jailer.** The chains that hold you back were built in your own mind. And the key to breaking free has been in your pocket all along.

Winning starts when you stop waiting for external solutions and take responsibility for your own transformation. This book will guide you, but no one can do the work for you.

So, ask yourself:

- What invisible chains have been holding you back?

- What false stories have you been telling yourself?

- Are you willing to break free and take control of your life?

If you truly commit to answering these questions, you've already taken the first step toward winning.

You will win—when you decide to.

Next Chapter: The Comfort Zone Trap

Now that you understand the invisible chains, we'll dive deeper into one of the strongest ones—the comfort zone. Why does it feel so safe? And how do you step out of it without fear? Let's explore in the next chapter.

Chapter 2: The Comfort Zone Trap

You've likely heard the phrase *"step out of your comfort zone."* But why is it so hard? Why do we cling to what is familiar, even when we know it's holding us back?

Your **comfort zone** is a psychological space where things feel safe and predictable. It's a mental boundary that keeps you from facing uncertainty, risk, or discomfort. But here's the problem: **Nothing grows in the comfort zone.** Every major breakthrough, success, or transformation happens outside of it.

Why We Stay in the Comfort Zone

The human brain is wired for **survival, not success**. It prefers routine, familiarity, and predictability. This is why new experiences—whether it's starting a business, moving to a new city, or speaking in public—can feel terrifying. Your brain interprets anything unfamiliar as a potential threat, even if logically, you know it won't harm you.

Here are some common reasons people stay in their comfort zones:

1. **Fear of failure** – *"What if I try and fail?"*

2. **Fear of judgment** – *"What will people say if I mess up?"*

3. **Fear of discomfort** – *"It's easier to stay where I am."*

4. **Lack of confidence** – *"I'm not ready yet."*

5. **The illusion of control** – *"If I don't take risks, I won't lose anything."*

What's interesting is that while the comfort zone feels safe, it's actually a **trap** that keeps you stagnant.

The Hidden Cost of Staying Comfortable

Imagine two people:

- **Emma**, who dreams of writing a book but never starts because she's afraid it won't be good enough.

- **James**, who wants to switch careers but stays in a job he hates because he's scared of uncertainty.

Both Emma and James believe they are avoiding discomfort, but in reality, they are choosing a **different kind of discomfort**—the regret of never trying.

What they don't realize is that staying in their comfort zone has a cost:

- Missed opportunities

- Lack of personal growth

- Unfulfilled potential

- The pain of regret

Ask yourself: *Which is scarier—trying and failing, or never trying and always wondering what could have been?*

Breaking Free from the Comfort Zone

So how do you escape this trap? You don't have to take giant leaps right away. The secret is to **expand** your comfort zone, step by step.

1. Start with Small Discomforts

Every big success starts with small actions. If you're afraid of public speaking, start by speaking up in meetings. If you want to start a business, take the first step—research, network, or test an idea.

- If you fear networking, start by introducing yourself to one new person a week.

- If you want to get fit but hate the gym, begin with a 10-minute walk every day.

These small actions **train your brain** to handle discomfort, making bigger steps easier.

2. Change Your Perspective on Fear

Fear is not the enemy—**inaction is**. Instead of seeing fear as a stop sign, see it as a green light. It means you're stepping into something new and growing.

Every successful person has felt fear. The difference is, they act **despite it**.

3. Get Comfortable with Failing

The only people who never fail are those who never try. Every failure teaches you something. If you adopt the mindset that **failure is feedback, not final**, you'll stop fearing it.

- **Thomas Edison** failed 10,000 times before inventing the light bulb.

- **Walt Disney** was fired from his first job for "lacking imagination."

- **J.K. Rowling** was rejected by 12 publishers before *Harry Potter* was accepted.

They all had one thing in common: they refused to stay in their comfort zones.

4. Create an Identity Shift

Stop saying, *"I'm just not the kind of person who takes risks."*

Instead, say, *"I am someone who grows, adapts, and takes action."*

Your identity shapes your behavior. If you believe you are the kind of person who steps out of their comfort zone, your actions will follow.

5. Set a 'Discomfort Challenge'

To truly break out of your comfort zone, challenge yourself to do something uncomfortable every day.

Here are a few examples:

- Speak up in a meeting.

- Try a new hobby you've always avoided.

- Start a conversation with a stranger.

- Wake up an hour earlier than usual.

- Ask for feedback, even if it's uncomfortable.

These small challenges **rewire your brain** to embrace discomfort rather than avoid it.

Real-Life Story: The Leap That Changed Everything

There was a man named David who had always been afraid of public speaking. The mere thought of standing in front of an audience made his hands sweat. For years, he avoided any situation where he might have to speak.

One day, he realized that his fear was controlling his life. So, he made a bold decision—he signed up for a **public speaking class**. The first session was terrifying, but he showed up. Then he signed up for another. And another.

Within a year, David was leading presentations at work. Within two years, he was delivering speeches to hundreds of people.

What changed? **He stopped waiting to feel "ready." He acted before he felt confident.**

Today, he laughs at the thought that he once let fear hold him back. His comfort zone expanded because he took action despite his fear.

Final Thought: Growth Lives Outside the Comfort Zone

The most successful, fulfilled, and confident people **are not fearless**—they have just learned to take action **despite their fears**.

The question is not whether stepping out of your comfort zone will be uncomfortable. It will be. The question is:

Are you willing to embrace that discomfort in exchange for growth, success, and self-confidence?

Remember:

- You don't have to take massive leaps—small steps will do.

- Fear doesn't mean stop—it means go.

- Discomfort is temporary, but regret lasts forever.

You **will** win—but only if you're willing to **step out of where you are and into who you're meant to be**.

Next Chapter: Fear of Failure – The Biggest Lie You Tell Yourself

Now that you understand the comfort zone trap, let's tackle the biggest reason people stay stuck—**the fear of failure**. What if failing wasn't the end, but the beginning of something great? Let's explore in the next chapter.

Chapter 3: Fear of Failure – The Biggest Lie You Tell Yourself

Failure. Just the word itself can trigger anxiety. It carries the weight of disappointment, embarrassment, and sometimes, even shame. From a young age, we're taught that failing is something to avoid at all costs. But what if I told you that **failure isn't your enemy—it's your greatest teacher?**

The fear of failure is **one of the biggest lies** we tell ourselves. It convinces us to play it safe, to avoid risks, and to never chase our dreams. But here's the truth: **Failure is not the opposite of success—it's a part of success.**

Why Are We So Afraid to Fail?

At its core, the fear of failure comes from two main sources:

1. **Social Conditioning** – From childhood, we're rewarded for getting things right and punished for getting things wrong. Schools grade us, workplaces evaluate us, and society admires winners while overlooking those who stumble. This trains us to fear mistakes instead of embracing them.
2. **Our Ego's Desire for Approval** – Many people don't actually fear failure itself; they fear what failure **looks like to others**. We don't want to be seen as incompetent, weak, or unsuccessful. So instead of trying and failing, we often choose not to try at all.

But by doing this, we guarantee something far worse than failure—**a life of regrets.**

Reframing Failure: What If It's a Stepping Stone?

Imagine a baby learning to walk. Does the baby fall? Yes. Does the baby cry sometimes? Sure. But does the baby ever decide, *"Maybe walking isn't for me. I should just crawl for the rest of my life."*? Absolutely not.

Yet as adults, we convince ourselves that failing once means we're not meant to succeed. But failure is **proof** that you are trying, growing, and moving forward.

Look at these real-life examples:

- **Michael Jordan** was cut from his high school basketball team. He later said, *"I have failed over and over and over again in my life. And that is why I succeed."*
- **Oprah Winfrey** was once fired from a television job for being "unfit for TV."
- **Walt Disney** was told he lacked imagination and had his first business go bankrupt before creating Disney.

What do they all have in common? **They didn't let failure define them. They let it refine them.**

The Hidden Cost of Avoiding Failure

Avoiding failure might seem like the safest path, but it has consequences:

1. **You Stay Stuck** – If you never risk failing, you also never risk growing. You remain in the same place while others move forward.
2. **You Live with Regret** – Years from now, you won't regret the things you tried and failed at. You'll regret the things you never dared to try.

3. **You Give Up Your Dreams** – Many people don't stop dreaming because they lack potential. They stop because they let the fear of failure kill their ambition.

Ask yourself: Is the fear of failure worth giving up your dreams?

How to Overcome the Fear of Failure

1. Change How You Define Failure

What if failure isn't **falling down** but **refusing to get back up**?

- **Wrong definition:** Failure means I'm not good enough.
- **Right definition:** Failure is feedback. It's a lesson that helps me improve.

Every time you fail, ask yourself: *What is this teaching me?*

2. Take Smaller Risks First

If you're terrified of failure, start small:

- If you fear public speaking, start by speaking up in small meetings.
- If you fear starting a business, begin with a small side project.

The more you expose yourself to controlled risks, the less fear controls you.

3. Separate Your Identity from Your Failures

Failing doesn't mean **you** are a failure. It simply means something didn't work.

If your first attempt at something fails, that doesn't mean you're not good enough. It just means you need to adjust your approach.

Failing is an event, not a person.

4. Use the 10-Year Test

Ask yourself:

- **Will this failure matter in 10 years?**
- **Will I even remember this mistake?**

Most failures feel huge in the moment but are insignificant in the long run. Don't let a temporary setback stop you from long-term success.

5. Look at the Worst-Case Scenario

Many people fear failure because they assume the worst. But take a moment to think—what's the absolute worst thing that could happen?

- If you apply for a job and don't get it, so what?
- If you start a business and it doesn't work, you'll learn valuable lessons.
- If you give a speech and forget your words, people will move on within minutes.

When you actually analyze the "worst case," you often realize it's not as bad as you thought.

A Real-Life Story: Learning to Embrace Failure

Ethan always wanted to start his own business. He had a great idea, but he kept hesitating. Every time he thought about launching, he told himself, *"What if I fail? What if people laugh at me?"*

Years passed, and he watched others succeed while he stayed in the same place. One day, he had a realization: **he was failing anyway—just in a different way.** By avoiding action, he was failing **without even trying**.

So he took the leap. He started his business. And guess what? His first attempt flopped. But instead of giving up, he learned. He made changes. And eventually, he succeeded.

Ethan's biggest lesson? *Failure wasn't nearly as scary as he had imagined. The only thing worse than failing was never trying at all.*

Final Thought: Fail Your Way to Success

The people who succeed in life aren't the ones who never fail. They're the ones who fail **more** than others—because they take more chances.

If you're afraid of failing, you're actually afraid of **learning**. And if you refuse to fail, you refuse to grow.

So here's the challenge:

- **Fail fast** – The quicker you fail, the quicker you learn.

- **Fail forward** – Each failure should push you closer to success.
- **Fail fearlessly** – Because the only real failure is **not trying at all**.

Success isn't about never falling—it's about getting up **one more time** than you fall.

Next Chapter: Self-Doubt and the Inner Critic

Now that you understand the truth about failure, let's address another major barrier: **self-doubt**. How do you silence that voice inside that tells you you're not good enough? Let's find out in the next chapter.

Chapter 4: Self-Doubt and the Inner Critic

There is a voice inside your head. You know the one—it whispers, *"You're not good enough."* It tells you, *"You don't have what it takes."* It reminds you of every mistake you've ever made and makes you question your worth.

This voice is your **inner critic**, and it is the root of self-doubt. If left unchecked, it can hold you back from opportunities, kill your confidence, and make you settle for less than you deserve.

But here's the truth: **That voice is lying to you.**

Where Does Self-Doubt Come From?

Self-doubt doesn't appear out of nowhere. It's the result of years of conditioning, experiences, and influences. Here are the most common sources:

1. **Past Failures** – If you've failed before, your brain reminds you of it every time you try something new.
2. **Negative Childhood Messages** – If you grew up hearing, *"You'll never succeed,"* or *"You're not as smart as others,"* those words can stay with you for years.
3. **Comparison** – Social media, family, and peers can make you feel like you're behind in life.
4. **Perfectionism** – If you believe you need to be perfect to be successful, you'll always feel like you're not good enough.
5. **Fear of Judgment** – Worrying about what others think can create self-doubt, making you hesitate instead of act.

The Truth About the Inner Critic

Imagine if a friend spoke to you the way your inner critic does. If they constantly said, *"You're not good enough,"* or *"You always fail,"* would you keep them in your life? Probably not.

So why do you let your inner critic talk to you this way?

The truth is, your **inner critic is not your enemy— it's a scared part of you trying to protect you.** It tries to stop you from taking risks, so you don't get hurt. But instead of keeping you safe, it keeps you **stuck**.

To win in life, you don't need to silence your inner critic completely. You just need to learn how to **manage it**.

How to Overcome Self-Doubt

1. Question the Voice

When your inner critic says, *"You're not good enough,"* challenge it:

- *Where is the proof that I'm not good enough?*
- *Is this a fact, or just an opinion I've accepted?*
- *What would I tell a friend who had this same thought?*

Most of the time, you'll realize there is **no real evidence** behind your self-doubt—it's just an old story you've been telling yourself.

2. Reframe the Narrative

Instead of thinking:

✗ *"I've never done this before, so I'll probably fail."*

Try:

☑️ *"I've never done this before, which means I'm about to learn something new."*

Your brain believes what you tell it. Start feeding it a better narrative.

3. Keep a 'Proof of Success' Journal

Every time you accomplish something—big or small—write it down.

- A compliment someone gave you.
- A challenge you overcame.
- A time when you doubted yourself but succeeded.

On days when self-doubt creeps in, read your journal. Remind yourself of **who you are** and **what you've already achieved**.

4. Take Action Before You Feel Ready

The biggest mistake people make is waiting to feel confident before taking action. But confidence doesn't come **before** action—it comes **after** it.

Think about learning to swim. If you waited until you *felt ready* to jump in the water, you would never start. But once you do, you realize it's not as scary as you thought.

Confidence is the same. The only way to silence self-doubt is to **prove it wrong through action**.

5. Stop Comparing Yourself to Others

Comparison is the fastest way to kill confidence. Social media makes it worse by showing highlight reels of other people's lives while hiding their struggles.

Instead of comparing yourself to others, compare yourself to **who you were yesterday**. Progress is personal—your only competition is your past self.

Real-Life Story: From Self-Doubt to Success

There was a woman named Emily who had always wanted to start her own clothing brand. But every time she thought about it, self-doubt crept in: *"What if no one buys it? What if I'm not good enough?"*

For years, she let that voice stop her. Until one day, she asked herself: **"What if I tried anyway?"**

She launched a small online store, and at first, sales were slow. But she didn't quit. She adjusted her designs, learned from her mistakes, and kept going. A year later, she was running a successful business.

When asked what changed, she said, *"I stopped believing the voice in my head. I realized that self-doubt never goes away—but you can succeed **despite** it."*

Final Thought: Your Inner Critic is Not the Truth

Self-doubt is just a voice—it is **not reality**. The only thing separating successful people from everyone else is that they **don't listen to their inner critic**. They feel doubt, but they act anyway.

So ask yourself:

- What would I do if I ignored self-doubt for one week?

- What dreams would I chase if I stopped believing my inner critic?
- What's one small action I can take today to prove my self-doubt wrong?

The only way to win is to **stop letting a false voice decide your future**.

Next Chapter: Procrastination – Your Dream Killer

Now that you know how to handle self-doubt, let's tackle another major barrier—**procrastination**. Why do we delay the things we know we need to do? And how do we break the cycle? Let's find out in the next chapter.

Chapter 5: Procrastination – Your Dream Killer

You know what you need to do. You've planned it, thought about it, maybe even set deadlines for it. But instead of starting, you find yourself scrolling through social media, watching one more episode, or telling yourself, *"I'll do it tomorrow."*

That's **procrastination**—the silent killer of dreams.

We often think of procrastination as just a bad habit, but it's much deeper than that. It's a **psychological trap** that keeps us stuck, delaying our goals and sabotaging our own success. But here's the truth: **Procrastination is not about laziness. It's about fear, doubt, and avoidance.**

Why Do We Procrastinate?

Most people assume procrastination happens because they're lazy or lack willpower. That's not true. Procrastination is actually a defense mechanism. Our brains are wired to **avoid discomfort and seek instant gratification**.

Here are the real reasons why you procrastinate:

1. **Fear of Failure** – If you never start, you can't fail. This way, you protect yourself from disappointment.
2. **Perfectionism** – You keep waiting for the "perfect time" or for things to be "just right" before taking action.
3. **Lack of Clarity** – You don't know where to start, so you keep putting it off.
4. **Overwhelm** – The task feels too big, so your brain avoids it altogether.

5. **Instant Gratification** – Watching TV or scrolling your phone feels good now, while work feels like effort.
6. **Self-Doubt** – You secretly question whether you can do it, so you delay starting.

Sound familiar? You're not alone. Procrastination affects even the most successful people—but the difference is, they've learned how to **overcome it**.

The Hidden Cost of Procrastination

Every time you procrastinate, you're making a choice. You're choosing **temporary comfort over long-term success**.

Think about it:

- If you keep putting off **exercising**, you'll remain out of shape.
- If you keep delaying **starting your business**, it will never happen.
- If you don't take action on **your dreams**, someone else will.

Procrastination **steals your future**—one delay at a time.

Imagine where you would be today if you had started six months ago. Now, imagine where you'll be six months from now if you **start today.**

How to Overcome Procrastination

1. Use the "Two-Minute Rule"

If a task feels overwhelming, break it down into something so small that it takes **two minutes or less** to start.

- Want to write a book? Write just **one sentence** today.
- Need to exercise? Do **one push-up**.
- Have a project? Open your laptop and set up the document.

Once you start, you'll find it easier to keep going. **Starting is the hardest part—just take the first step.**

2. The 5-Second Rule

Mel Robbins, a motivational speaker, created the **5-Second Rule**:

"If you have an instinct to act on a goal, count down 5-4-3-2-1, then do it before your brain talks you out of it."

Your mind will always try to make excuses. This simple trick **overrides hesitation** and pushes you into action.

3. Work in Short Bursts

Instead of telling yourself you need to work for hours, commit to just **25 minutes** of focused work using the **Pomodoro Technique**:

- Work for 25 minutes.
- Take a 5-minute break.
- Repeat.

This keeps your mind fresh and makes big tasks feel manageable.

4. Make It Public

Tell someone about your goal. When you have **external accountability**, you're less likely to procrastinate.

- Want to write a book? Announce it to your friends.
- Need to lose weight? Get a workout partner.
- Starting a business? Share your progress online.

When others are watching, you'll feel more pressure to follow through.

5. Focus on Progress, Not Perfection

Perfectionism is one of the biggest causes of procrastination. You keep telling yourself, *"I'll start when I'm ready,"* but that "perfect moment" never comes.

Remember: **Done is better than perfect.** The sooner you start, the sooner you can improve.

A Real-Life Story: Beating Procrastination

Jack had always wanted to start a YouTube channel. He had the equipment, the ideas, and the passion. But every time he thought about filming, he found an excuse: *"I need better lighting,"* or *"I don't have time today."*

Months went by. Then a year.

One day, Jack decided to apply the **Two-Minute Rule.** Instead of trying to film a perfect video, he committed to recording **just one minute.** That small action led to another. Soon, he had his first video uploaded.

Now, his channel has thousands of followers. And when asked what changed, he said: *"I stopped waiting for the perfect time and just started."*

Final Thought: Procrastination is a Choice

You have two choices:

1. Keep waiting for the "right moment" and stay in the same place.
2. Take action today, even if it's small, and start moving forward.

No matter how big your goal is, **starting is always the hardest part.** But once you begin, momentum takes over.

So ask yourself: **What is one small thing you can do today to take action?**

Because here's the truth: **You will win—but only if you stop delaying and start doing.**

Next Chapter: Excuses vs. Reality – Facing the Truth

Now that you understand procrastination, let's tackle the next barrier: **Excuses**. Why do we create them, and how do we break free from them? Let's dive in.

Chapter 6: Excuses vs. Reality – Facing the Truth

We all do it.

- *"I don't have time."*

- *"I'm too old."*

- *"I don't have the right skills."*

- *"It's not the right moment."*

Excuses. They sound logical. They feel real. But in most cases, **excuses are just lies we tell ourselves to avoid discomfort.**

The truth? **Your excuses are not stopping you— your mindset is.**

The Real Reason We Make Excuses

Excuses are a defense mechanism. They protect us from the fear of failure, judgment, and discomfort.

Here's why people make excuses:

1. **Fear of Failure** – If you don't try, you can't fail.

2. **Fear of Success** – Some people fear the responsibility that comes with winning.

3. **Lack of Confidence** – Deep down, they don't believe they can succeed.

4. **Avoiding Discomfort** – Change is hard, so they justify staying the same.

5. **Perfectionism** – They wait for the "perfect" conditions that never come.

Excuses are comforting, but they **steal your future.**

Common Excuses and the Truth Behind Them

Let's break down some of the most common excuses:

Excuse #1: "I don't have time."

Reality: You have time for what you make a priority.

Think about how much time you spend:

- Scrolling through social media

- Watching TV

- Doing things that don't bring you closer to your goals

Successful people don't have more hours in a day than you. They just **use their time differently.**

Solution: Track your time for a week. Identify time-wasters and replace them with productive habits.

Excuse #2: "I don't have the money."

Reality: You don't need money to start—you need **resourcefulness**.

Many successful businesses started with little or no money. What they lacked in cash, they made up for in:

- Skills

- Creativity

- Persistence

Solution: Start with what you have. Learn skills online for free. Network. Find ways to make it work.

Excuse #3: "I'm not ready yet."

Reality: You'll never feel 100% ready.

Read that again.

No one starts as an expert. Every master was once a beginner. The only way to become ready is to start before you feel ready.

Solution: Take the first small step today. Perfection comes from progress, not waiting.

Excuse #4: "I'm too old."

Reality: Success has no age limit.

- **Colonel Sanders** started KFC at 65.

- **Vera Wang** designed her first dress at 40.

- **Ray Kroc** founded McDonald's at 52.

It's never too late. The only thing stopping you is **belief**.

Solution: Focus on **what you can do today** instead of what you didn't do yesterday.

Excuse #5: "I don't have the right connections."

Reality: You can build connections.

No one is born with a network. Every successful person built their relationships over time.

Solution:

- Reach out to people in your industry.

- Attend events or join online communities.

- Add value to others before expecting anything in return.

The right connections come when you put yourself out there.

The Price of Excuses

Every excuse has a cost.

- The cost of **staying in the same place.**

- The cost of **wasted time and potential.**

- The cost of **watching others succeed while you stand still.**

Excuses feel safe, but they come at the price of your **dreams.**

Now ask yourself:

- *Where would I be if I stopped making excuses six months ago?*

- *What could I achieve if I stopped making excuses today?*

How to Break Free from Excuses

1. Take Full Responsibility

No more blaming your past, your circumstances, or other people. The moment you take full responsibility for your life, **you take back control.**

2. Replace Excuses with Action

Instead of saying, *"I can't,"* ask: *"How can I?"*

- Instead of *"I don't have time,"* say *"I will make time."*

- Instead of *"I don't know how,"* say *"I will learn."*

Your words shape your mindset.

3. Commit to One Small Change

Pick **one** excuse you've been making. Replace it with action **right now**.

- If you say, *"I don't have time to exercise,"* do 10 push-ups right now.

- If you say, *"I don't have money to start a business,"* research free ways to start.

Small actions lead to momentum.

Real-Life Story: From Excuses to Success

Mark always wanted to write a book, but for years, he told himself:

- *"I don't have time."*

- *"I'm not a great writer."*

- *"I don't know where to start."*

Then one day, he asked himself: *"What if I stop making excuses and just write one page?"*

That one page turned into two. Then five. Then ten.

A year later, his book was published.

Mark's success didn't come from waiting for the perfect moment—it came from **stopping the excuses and taking action.**

Final Thought: No More Excuses

The difference between people who succeed and people who don't?

Successful people **find a way**. Others find an excuse.

So, which one will you choose?

You will win—when you stop making excuses and start making progress.

Next Chapter: Perfectionism – When Good Is Never Enough

Now that we've eliminated excuses, let's tackle another hidden barrier—**perfectionism**. What if trying to be perfect is the very thing keeping you from success? Let's explore in the next chapter.

Chapter 7: Perfectionism – When Good Is Never Enough

Perfectionism sounds like a strength. After all, isn't it good to set high standards? Isn't striving for excellence the key to success?

Yes—but only **if it doesn't paralyze you.**

The problem with perfectionism is that it doesn't push you forward—it **holds you back.** Instead of helping you succeed, it creates fear, delays action, and makes you feel like you're never good enough. **Perfectionism doesn't lead to progress—it leads to procrastination and self-doubt.**

The Perfectionism Trap

Perfectionists often think they're just being "careful" or "detail-oriented." But in reality, they are trapped in a cycle of:

1. **Setting unrealistic expectations** – Everything must be flawless, or it's a failure.

2. **Procrastinating** – Since they can't do it perfectly, they delay starting.

3. **Over-editing and overthinking** – They constantly tweak, revise, and obsess over small details.

4. **Never feeling satisfied** – Even when they achieve something, they feel it could have been better.

5. **Burning out** – The pressure to be perfect is exhausting.

If you find yourself stuck in this cycle, it's time to break free.

Signs You Might Be a Perfectionist

- You delay starting projects because you don't feel "ready" yet.

- You spend hours obsessing over tiny details that no one else notices.

- You're afraid of criticism because it feels like personal failure.

- You avoid taking risks unless you're sure you'll succeed.

- You struggle to finish things because they never feel "good enough."

Sound familiar? **You're not alone.** Perfectionism affects millions of people, but the good news is—you can overcome it.

The Hidden Cost of Perfectionism

Perfectionism is a **dream killer**. Here's why:

1. **It Delays Action** – You spend so much time planning that you never actually do anything.

2. **It Creates Fear of Failure** – You avoid trying because you're afraid of making mistakes.

3. **It Stops You from Growing** – If you only do things you're already great at, you never develop new skills.

4. **It Steals Joy** – Even when you achieve something, you don't celebrate because it's "not perfect."

Here's a question: *Would you rather have an imperfect book, business, or goal completed, or a perfect idea that never sees the light of day?*

Done is always better than perfect.

How to Overcome Perfectionism

1. Set Progress Goals, Not Perfection Goals

Instead of aiming for "flawless," aim for **consistent progress**.

- Instead of *"I have to write the perfect book,"* say *"I will write 500 words every day."*

- Instead of *"I need to master this skill before I start,"* say *"I will practice daily and improve as I go."*

Your goal should be **growth, not perfection.**

2. Set a "Good Enough" Deadline

Give yourself **a time limit** to complete tasks.

- **Writing an article?** Give yourself two hours, then hit publish.

- **Launching a business?** Set a launch date and stick to it.

Perfectionists keep **tweaking** and **revising** forever. A deadline forces you to move forward.

3. Embrace Imperfection as a Teacher

Mistakes are not proof that you're failing—they're proof that you're learning.

Every successful person has failed **more times than others have even tried, again,**

- **Thomas Edison** had thousands of failed experiments before inventing the lightbulb.

- **Elon Musk** had multiple failed companies before Tesla and SpaceX succeeded.

- **J.K. Rowling** was rejected by 12 publishers before *Harry Potter* became a global hit.

They didn't wait for perfection—they acted, learned, and adjusted. **You should too.**

4. The 80% Rule: If It's 80% Good, It's Ready

The biggest secret of successful people? **They launch at 80% and improve as they go.**

- The first iPhone wasn't perfect—it had flaws. Apple released it anyway and improved in later versions.

- The first version of Facebook was simple, ugly, and full of bugs. It still changed the world.

If you wait for perfection, **you'll never start.** Instead, launch at 80%, get feedback, and improve over time.

5. Celebrate Small Wins

Perfectionists only celebrate **final results**, which means they rarely feel successful.

Instead, celebrate every step forward.

- Wrote one page? That's progress.

- Finished a rough draft? That's a win.

- Made your first sale? That's momentum.

Success is built on small victories.

Real-Life Story: The Power of Imperfect Action

Emma always wanted to start a blog. But every time she tried, she stopped herself with thoughts like:

- *"My writing isn't good enough."*

- *"I don't have a perfect website."*

- *"I need more experience before I start."*

Years passed. Then one day, she decided to **just start**— even if her blog wasn't perfect.

Her first posts were messy. Her website wasn't great. But **she kept going.**

Within a year, she had thousands of readers. Within two years, she turned her blog into a full-time business.

Emma's success didn't come from **waiting for perfection**—it came from **taking action despite imperfection**.

Final Thought: Let Go of Perfect, Start Winning

Perfectionism is just fear in disguise.

- **Waiting for the perfect time?** It won't come.

- **Waiting until you're 100% ready?** You never will be.

- **Waiting to feel confident?** Confidence comes from **doing, not waiting.**

You will win—not by being perfect, but by taking action despite imperfection.

Next Chapter: The Paralysis of Overthinking

Now that you know perfectionism is a trap, let's tackle another major roadblock—**overthinking.** Why do we get stuck in endless loops of doubt, and how do we break free? Let's explore in the next chapter.

Chapter 8: The Paralysis of Overthinking

Have you ever caught yourself analyzing a situation so much that you end up doing nothing? You think about every possible outcome, weigh every decision, and before you know it—you're stuck.

This is **overthinking**, and it's one of the biggest reasons people fail to take action. It makes small problems seem bigger, simple decisions feel impossible, and turns dreams into endless "what ifs."

Why Do We Overthink?

Overthinking is a trap set by your brain to **keep you in your comfort zone.** Your mind convinces you that by thinking more, you're making progress—but in reality, you're just delaying action.

Here's why we do it:

1. **Fear of Making the Wrong Choice** – You don't want to make a mistake, so you keep analyzing every possibility.

2. **Lack of Confidence** – You don't trust yourself, so you keep seeking more information.

3. **Desire for Control** – You want to predict every outcome before taking action.

4. **Perfectionism** – You feel like you need all the answers before you start.

But overthinking doesn't lead to better decisions—it leads to **paralysis**.

The Problem with Overthinking

Overthinking feels productive, but it actually **stops you from moving forward.**

- Instead of **starting your business**, you spend months researching and never launch.

- Instead of **asking for a promotion**, you overanalyze every conversation and never make your move.

- Instead of **starting a project**, you question every detail and end up doing nothing.

Overthinking steals your time, energy, and opportunities. The longer you think, the less you act.

And without action, you cannot win.

How to Break Free from Overthinking

1. Use the "Two-Minute Rule"

If a decision takes **less than two minutes** to make, **decide immediately.**

- Should I go to the gym? **Yes.**

- Should I call that client? **Yes.**

- Should I start writing today? **Yes.**

Most decisions don't need hours of thinking—**they need action.**

2. Set a Decision Deadline

Give yourself a **fixed time limit** to make a decision.

- If you're choosing between two options, **give yourself 24 hours** to decide.

- If you're overthinking an email, **give yourself 5 minutes** to write and send it.

- If you're debating a business move, **set a deadline and commit.**

Indecision is worse than making the wrong choice. At least when you decide, you learn.

3. Limit Your Information Intake

Many people overthink because they feel like they need **more information.** But in reality, more information **doesn't always lead to better decisions—it leads to more doubt.**

- Set a **limit** on how much research you do.

- Trust yourself to make a decision based on what you already know.

- Remember: **You don't need ALL the answers—you just need to start.**

4. Ask Yourself: What's the Worst That Can Happen?

Overthinking makes problems seem **bigger than they really are.**

Ask yourself:

- What's the worst that could happen if I make the wrong choice?

- Will this decision even matter in **five years**?

- Is it worth spending days worrying about this?

Most of the time, the "worst-case scenario" is not as bad as you imagine. And even if it happens, **you can handle it.**

5. Take Imperfect Action

The best way to stop overthinking? **Act before you feel ready.**

- Instead of **planning** to start a business, sell your first product.

- Instead of **thinking** about writing a book, write the first page.

- Instead of **worrying** about your speech, practice it once and adjust later.

Action beats overthinking **every time.**

Real-Life Story: The Power of Quick Decisions

David always wanted to start a podcast. He spent months researching the best microphones, editing software, and branding. But the more he researched, the more overwhelmed he felt.

One day, he decided to stop **thinking** and start **doing**. He recorded his first episode on his phone—no fancy equipment, no perfect script.

Was it perfect? No. But it was **done**.

Today, David's podcast has thousands of listeners—not because he overanalyzed, but because he **took action.**

Final Thought: Overthinking is the Enemy of Winning

Every second you spend overthinking is a second you **could be making progress.**

- **Stop thinking. Start doing.**

- **Make decisions faster.**

- **Trust yourself to figure things out along the way.**

You will win **when you stop letting overthinking slow you down.**

Next Chapter: Comparing Yourself to Others – A Losing Game

Now that we've tackled overthinking, let's address another major barrier—**comparison.** Why do we constantly compare ourselves to others, and how can we break free from it? Let's find out in the next chapter.

Chapter 9: Comparing Yourself to Others – A Losing Game

Have you ever scrolled through social media and thought, *Why am I so far behind?* Maybe you see someone traveling the world, landing their dream job, or building a successful business, and suddenly, your own progress feels insignificant.

This is **comparison syndrome**, and it's a trap.

Comparing yourself to others doesn't inspire growth—it **steals your confidence, joy, and motivation.** It makes you feel like you're not doing enough, not achieving enough, and worst of all—not enough as a person.

But here's the truth: **Comparison is a losing game, because you're measuring yourself against someone else's highlight reel.**

Why Do We Compare Ourselves?

Comparison is a natural human instinct. Thousands of years ago, comparing ourselves to others helped us **survive**—we learned from the strongest hunters, the best farmers, and the wisest leaders.

But today, comparison doesn't help us survive—it makes us miserable.

Here's why we compare:

1. **Social Media Illusion** – We only see the best moments of people's lives, not their struggles.

2. **Fear of Falling Behind** – Society pushes the idea that you should achieve certain milestones by a certain age.

3. **Self-Doubt** – When you don't believe in yourself, you look at others to measure your worth.

4. **Perfectionism** – You believe you have to be "as good as" someone else to succeed.

But here's the problem—**comparison is never fair. You're** comparing your behind-the-scenes **struggles** to someone else's **best moments.**

The Hidden Cost of Comparison

The more you compare, the more you:

- **Lose motivation** – Instead of working on your own path, you waste time watching others.

- **Feel unworthy** – You believe you're not good enough because someone else seems ahead.

- **Live for approval** – You start chasing what *looks* successful, instead of what *feels* right for you.

And worst of all? **Comparison makes you forget your own unique path.**

The truth is, **there is no race.** Success is not a one-size-fits-all journey. The only person you need to be better than is **who you were yesterday.**

How to Stop Comparing Yourself to Others

1. Compare Yourself to Your Past, Not to Others

Instead of asking, *"Am I as successful as them?"* ask, *"Am I better than I was a year ago?"*

Track your **own** growth. Celebrate your **own** wins. Measure progress based on **your own** journey.

2. Limit Social Media Consumption

Social media is designed to show people's **best moments, not their struggles.**

- No one posts their failures.

- No one shares their insecurities.

- No one shows the nights they cried over self-doubt.

Solution: Take breaks from social media. Follow people who inspire, not discourage.

3. Focus on Your Strengths

You will always find someone who is better at something than you. But guess what? **They are not YOU.**

Instead of wishing for someone else's skills, ask:

- *What am I great at?*

- *What do I love doing?*

- *What makes me unique?*

Play **your own game.** Stay in **your own lane.**

4. Turn Comparison into Inspiration

Instead of feeling jealous, **learn from people who are ahead of you.**

- Instead of saying, *"I'll never be as successful as them,"* ask, *"What can I learn from them?"*

- Instead of feeling defeated, **study their journey** and apply what works for you.

Use **admiration as fuel, not as self-doubt.**

5. Remind Yourself: No One Has It All Together

Even the most successful people struggle.

- The millionaire you admire might have broken relationships.

- The fitness model you follow might have body image issues.

- The famous entrepreneur might battle anxiety every day.

No one's life is perfect. **Everyone has struggles—you just don't see them.**

Real-Life Story: Winning by Focusing on Your Own Journey

Chris was a young entrepreneur who spent years comparing himself to others. He followed influencers who seemed to have everything—money, success, and a dream life.

Every time he saw their posts, he felt **less**. He believed he wasn't successful enough, smart enough, or rich enough.

One day, he made a decision—**to stop looking at others and start focusing on his own journey.**

He set his own goals. He stopped scrolling endlessly. He tracked his own progress.

A year later, his business took off. And when asked what changed, he said: *"I stopped competing with others and started competing with myself."*

That's the secret. **The only competition that matters is the one with yourself.**

Final Thought: Stay in Your Own Lane

If you run a race looking at the person next to you, **you'll trip.**

If you focus on your own lane, **you'll win.**

- **Success is not about being better than others—it's about being better than yesterday.**

- **Your path is different. Your timeline is different. Your success is yours alone.**

- **The only person stopping you is you.**

Stop comparing. **Start building your own success.**

Next Chapter: The Role of Negative Influences in Your Life

Now that we've tackled comparison, let's address another silent barrier—**negative influences.** How do the people around you shape your success? And how do you protect yourself from toxic energy? Let's find out in the next chapter.

Chapter 10: The Role of Negative Influences in Your Life

Look around you. The people you spend time with, the content you consume, and the conversations you engage in—**all of these shape your mindset, your confidence, and ultimately, your success.**

Ever heard the saying, *"You are the average of the five people you spend the most time with"*? It's true. The energy, beliefs, and habits of those around you either **push you forward or pull you back.**

The problem is, many people don't realize how much negative influences are weighing them down—until it's too late.

How Negative Influences Hold You Back

Negative influences come in different forms. Some are obvious. Others are more subtle.

Here's how they show up in your life:

1. **Toxic People** – The ones who criticize, belittle, or discourage your dreams.

2. **Energy Drainers** – People who constantly complain, gossip, or bring negativity into your space.

3. **Naysayers** – The ones who say, *"That's impossible,"* or *"You'll never succeed."*

4. **Comfort-Zone Friends** – People who fear change and pressure you to stay the same.

5. **Social Media Comparison** – Constantly consuming content that makes you feel like you're not good enough.

6. **Limiting Beliefs from Family or Society** – Messages like, *"People like us don't succeed,"* or *"Be realistic."*

These influences create **self-doubt, hesitation, and fear**—even when you don't realize it.

If you're surrounded by negativity, it doesn't matter how motivated you are—**you will struggle to move forward.**

Signs That You're Surrounded by Negative Influences

- You feel **drained** after spending time with certain people.

- You hear more **criticism** than encouragement.

- You constantly **doubt yourself** because of what others say.

- You feel **guilty** for wanting to grow or change.

- You find yourself **playing small** to fit in.

If any of these sound familiar, it's time to **protect your energy.**

How to Remove Negative Influences

1. Identify Who (or What) is Holding You Back

Make a list of people, environments, or habits that bring negativity into your life.

- Are there people who constantly doubt you?

- Do you engage in negative conversations?

- Are you consuming toxic content on social media?

Awareness is the first step to change.

2. Set Boundaries with Negative People

You don't have to cut people off completely—but you **do** need boundaries.

- If someone always complains, change the subject or limit conversations.

- If a friend discourages you, stop sharing your dreams with them.

- If someone disrespects you, **speak up or distance yourself.**

Your energy is **precious**—protect it.

3. Spend More Time with Positive Influences

Surround yourself with people who:
✓ Encourage your growth

✓ Support your goals
✓ Push you to be better
✓ Inspire you with their actions

If you don't have these people in your life yet, **seek them out.** Join groups, attend events, and connect with like-minded individuals.

The right environment will transform you.

4. Control What You Consume

It's not just people—it's also what you read, watch, and listen to.

- Replace **negative news** with uplifting content.

- Unfollow accounts that make you feel **insecure or stuck.**

- Read books, listen to podcasts, and watch videos that **motivate and educate you.**

Your mind is like a sponge—**feed it positivity.**

5. Believe That You Deserve Better

Many people tolerate negative influences because they believe they **have to.**

- *"I've known them forever."*

- *"They're family—I can't avoid them."*

- *"I don't want to be rude."*

But here's the truth: **You don't owe anyone access to your energy.**

You are allowed to **outgrow** negative relationships. You are allowed to **prioritize your mental health.**

You **deserve** to be surrounded by people who make you better.

Real-Life Story: Cutting Out Negativity to Succeed

Daniel always dreamed of starting his own business. But every time he talked about it, his friends laughed.

- *"That's risky. You should just stick to your job."*

- *"Most businesses fail, you know."*

- *"You're not the type of person to do that."*

For years, their words held him back. He doubted himself. He played it safe.

One day, Daniel made a decision—**to stop listening to negativity.**

He spent less time with doubters and more time with successful entrepreneurs. He read books, took courses, and surrounded himself with people who believed in him.

A year later, he launched his business. Today, it's thriving.

When asked what changed, he said: *"I didn't just change my mindset—I changed my environment."*

Final Thought: Your Environment Shapes Your Success

- **If you surround yourself with doubt, you will doubt yourself.**

- **If you surround yourself with winners, you will think like a winner.**

Take control of your influences. **Cut out negativity. Seek inspiration. Build a circle that lifts you higher.**

You will win—but only when you stop letting negative energy hold you back.

Next Chapter: Mindset Matters – How to Think Like a Winner

Now that we've cleared out negativity, it's time to rewire your mindset. How do successful people think differently? And how can you develop a winning mentality? Let's explore in the next chapter.

Section 2:
Rewiring Your Mindset

Chapter 11: Mindset Matters – How to Think Like a Winner

Success is not just about talent, luck, or even hard work. **It starts in your mind.**

Winners don't think like everyone else. They see challenges differently, handle failures differently, and approach opportunities with a different perspective.

The truth is, **your thoughts shape your reality.** If you think like a winner, you'll start acting like one. But if you think like a loser—always doubting, hesitating, and expecting failure—you'll create a life that reflects those beliefs.

The Power of Your Mindset

Your mindset is the filter through which you see the world. It determines:

✔ How you handle setbacks
✔ Whether you take action or hesitate
✔ How you see yourself and your abilities

Two people can face the **same** situation but have completely **different** outcomes—all because of mindset.

The Difference Between a Winning and Losing Mindset

A **winning mindset** helps you grow, take action, and move forward. A **losing mindset** keeps you stuck in fear and excuses. Here's how they differ:

✓ **Winners see failure as a lesson.**
✗ Losers see failure as proof they're not good enough.

✓ **Winners believe they'll figure things out.**
✗ Losers believe they need all the answers before they start.

✓ **Winners embrace challenges because they make them stronger.**
✗ Losers avoid challenges because they fear struggle.

✓ **Winners know success takes time and effort.**
✗ Losers give up when they don't see fast results.

✓ **Winners take full responsibility for their actions.**
✗ Losers blame others, circumstances, or bad luck.

See the difference? **One mindset leads to growth. The other leads to excuses.**

How to Develop a Winning Mindset

1. Reframe Problems as Opportunities

Winners see **challenges** as a chance to grow.

Instead of saying, *"This is too hard,"* ask:

✓ *"What can I learn from this?"*
✓ *"How can this make me stronger?"*

Every setback is a lesson. Every obstacle is a test of your commitment.

2. Take Full Responsibility for Your Life

The moment you say, *"It's not my fault,"* you give away your power.

✓ Winners take **ownership** of their decisions, actions, and future.
✗ Losers wait for luck, blame circumstances, and make excuses.

Your life is in your hands. The day you stop blaming and start **owning your choices**, everything changes.

3. Focus on Growth, Not Perfection

Perfectionists often fail—not because they're not capable, but because they're **too afraid to start.**

✓ **Winners focus on progress, not perfection.** They take action, make mistakes, and improve along the way.
✗ **Losers wait until everything is perfect.** As a result, they never start.

Done is better than perfect. Take action now—refine later.

4. Control Your Inner Voice

Your thoughts become your reality. If you constantly think, *"I'm not good enough,"* you'll act in ways that prove it true.

Instead, start replacing negative thoughts with empowering ones:

✗ *"I can't do this."* → ✓ *"I may not know how yet, but I can learn."*
✗ *"I always fail."* → ✓ *"Failure is part of my success story."*
✗ *"I'm not lucky."* → ✓ *"I create my own opportunities."*

Your mind listens to what you tell it. **Feed it winning thoughts.**

5. Surround Yourself with Winners

Your environment shapes your mindset.

✓ **Winners surround themselves with positive, ambitious people.**
✗ **Losers spend time with complainers, doubters, and excuse-makers.**

If you want to think like a winner, **spend time with winners.** Seek out people who inspire, challenge, and push you to grow.

Real-Life Story: The Mindset Shift That Changed Everything

James was stuck in a cycle of failure. Every time something went wrong, he blamed his past, his family, or bad luck.

One day, he read a quote: **"Your thoughts create your reality."**

That hit him hard. He realized he had spent years thinking like a loser—and as a result, he was living like one.

So he made a shift:
✓ He stopped making excuses.
✓ He took control of his choices.
✓ He started seeing every challenge as an opportunity.

Fast forward two years—James owns a successful business. He credits one thing: **changing his mindset.**

Final Thought: Your Mindset = Your Future

Your success or failure in life comes down to **one thing—how you think.**

✓ If you think like a **winner**, you'll act like one.
✗ If you think like a **loser**, you'll stay stuck.

Your **thoughts create your reality.** Choose them wisely.

You will win—but only if you train your mind to think like a winner.

Next Chapter: Growth vs. Fixed Mindset – Choosing the Path to Success

Now that you understand the power of mindset, let's go deeper. What's the difference between a **growth mindset** and a **fixed mindset**? And how can shifting your mindset change your life? Let's explore in the next chapter.

Chapter 12: Growth vs. Fixed Mindset – Choosing the Path to Success

Why do some people keep improving while others stay stuck? Why do some bounce back from failure, while others give up at the first obstacle?

The answer is **mindset.**

There are two types of mindsets that shape everything in your life:

✓ **A Growth Mindset** – The belief that you can improve, learn, and develop through effort.
✗ **A Fixed Mindset** – The belief that your abilities, intelligence, and talents are set in stone.

The mindset you choose determines your success, resilience, and overall happiness.

The Difference Between a Growth and Fixed Mindset

✓ **People with a Growth Mindset believe:**

- *"I can learn anything with effort."*

- *"Challenges make me stronger."*

- *"Failure is a stepping stone, not the end."*

- *"Skills can be developed with practice."*

- *"Hard work beats talent when talent doesn't work hard."*

✗ People with a Fixed Mindset believe:

- *"I'm either good at something or I'm not."*

- *"If I fail, it means I'm not talented."*

- *"I avoid challenges because I might look bad."*

- *"I can't improve—I'm just not that kind of person."*

- *"Successful people were born that way."*

Do you see the difference? One mindset **empowers** you, while the other **limits** you.

Why a Growth Mindset Leads to Success

People with a **growth mindset** achieve more because they:

✓ **Take more action** – They don't wait to be "naturally talented"; they develop skills through practice.
✓ **Bounce back from failure** – They see setbacks as learning experiences, not reasons to quit.
✓ **Push beyond their comfort zone** – They embrace challenges as opportunities to grow.
✓ **Become unstoppable** – They don't let self-doubt hold them back because they know improvement is always possible.

Your success in any area—career, relationships, health—depends on whether you choose a growth or fixed mindset.

How to Develop a Growth Mindset

1. Reframe Failure as Feedback

✗ Fixed Mindset: *"I failed. That means I'm not good enough."*
✓ Growth Mindset: *"I failed. That means I'm learning."*

Failure is not a dead-end—it's a stepping stone. **Every mistake teaches you something valuable.**

- If you fail a test, study differently next time.

- If your business idea flops, analyze what went wrong and improve.

- If you struggle with a skill, practice more instead of quitting.

Failure only becomes permanent when you stop trying.

2. Replace "I Can't" with "I Can't... Yet"

The word **"yet"** is powerful. It shifts your mindset from limitation to possibility.

✗ Fixed Mindset: *"I can't start a business."*
✓ Growth Mindset: *"I can't start a business... yet. But I can learn."*

✗ Fixed Mindset: *"I'm not good at public speaking."*
✓ Growth Mindset: *"I'm not good at public speaking... yet. But I can improve."*

Adding **"yet"** reminds you that **skills can be built over time.**

3. Challenge Yourself Daily

People with a growth mindset seek **constant improvement.**

- **Learn a new skill.** Read, take a course, or practice something you're weak at.

- **Step out of your comfort zone.** If something scares you, that's a sign you should do it.

- **Take on challenges instead of avoiding them.** Struggle = Growth.

Every day is an opportunity to improve—even 1% at a time.

4. Surround Yourself with Growth-Minded People

Your mindset is shaped by the people around you.

✓ **Growth-Minded Circle:** People who push you to grow, challenge you, and support your ambitions.
✗ **Fixed-Minded Circle:** People who complain, avoid challenges, and discourage your dreams.

If you want to **think bigger, grow stronger, and achieve more**, surround yourself with people who have a **growth mindset**.

5. Focus on Effort, Not Just Talent

Many people believe success comes from talent alone—but that's a **fixed mindset**.

✓ Growth-minded people know that effort is the real key to success.

- **Michael Jordan** was cut from his high school basketball team but became the greatest because he outworked everyone.

- **Oprah Winfrey** was told she wasn't fit for TV, but she didn't quit—she kept improving.

- **Elon Musk** wasn't born a genius—he read books, learned, and took action.

Talent gives you a head start, but **effort is what takes you to the finish line.**

Real-Life Story: The Growth Mindset Transformation

Lisa always struggled with math. She believed she was "just bad at numbers." Every time she saw a math problem, she thought, *"I'm not a math person."*

Then, she learned about the **growth mindset** and decided to challenge her belief.

✓ She stopped saying, *"I'm bad at math."* Instead, she said, *"I just need more practice."*

✓ She studied a little every day instead of avoiding it.

✓ She stopped focusing on getting every answer right and started focusing on **improving**.

Fast forward a year—Lisa aced her math exams. Not because she suddenly became a "math person," but because she **shifted her mindset**.

Final Thought: Your Mindset Shapes Your Future

✓ **Every skill can be learned.**

✓ **Every challenge makes you stronger.**

✓ **Every failure is a lesson, not a limit.**

Success is not about what you're born with—it's about the mindset you choose.

You will win—but only if you believe that you can grow, improve, and become better every single day.

Next Chapter: Resilience – Turning Setbacks Into Comebacks

Now that you understand the power of mindset, let's talk about **resilience**. How do winners bounce back from failure? How can you turn setbacks into comebacks? Let's find out in the next chapter.

Chapter 13: Resilience – Turning Setbacks Into Comebacks

Life will knock you down. That's a guarantee.

But the difference between **winners and quitters** isn't who avoids failure—it's **who gets back up.**

Resilience is the ability to recover, adapt, and keep moving forward despite challenges. It's what separates those who achieve success from those who give up at the first sign of difficulty.

The truth is, **you will face obstacles.** The question is, *will you let them stop you, or will you use them as fuel to push forward?*

Why Resilience is the Key to Success

Everyone wants an easy road to success, but that's not how it works. If you study any highly successful person, you'll notice one thing:

✓ They **failed** many times.
✓ They **faced rejection and setbacks.**
✓ They **kept going when most people quit.**

What makes someone successful is not **avoiding failure,** but **learning how to recover from it.**

The Truth About Setbacks

✗ Most people see failure as proof that they're not good enough.
✓ Resilient people see failure as feedback and a necessary step to growth.

Think about it this way: **If you never fall, how will you learn to stand up stronger?**

Every setback carries a lesson:

- A failed business teaches you what **not to do** next time.

- A lost job forces you to develop new skills and find better opportunities.

- A rejected idea makes you refine and improve before trying again.

Resilience is not about avoiding struggles—it's about using them to your advantage.

How to Build Unshakable Resilience

1. Reframe Failure as a Lesson

Instead of thinking:

✗ *"This didn't work, so I'm not meant for success."*
Start thinking:
✓ *"This didn't work, so now I know what to improve."*

Every failure contains **valuable data**—it tells you what needs adjusting. The faster you learn, the faster you grow.

2. Control What You Can, Let Go of What You Can't

Many people waste energy worrying about things **outside their control**—the economy, other people's opinions, luck.

✓ Winners focus on what they CAN control:

- Their effort

- Their mindset

- Their response to challenges

When something goes wrong, ask yourself: *"What CAN I do right now?"* Then do it.

3. Develop Mental Toughness

Resilience isn't about being unaffected by failure—it's about **handling failure without breaking down.**

Ways to build mental strength:
✓ Do hard things on purpose – Challenge yourself daily, even in small ways.
✓ Practice self-discipline – Show up even when you don't feel like it.
✓ Get comfortable with discomfort – Growth happens outside your comfort zone.

The stronger your mind, the easier it becomes to bounce back.

4. Use Setbacks as Motivation

Some people use failure as a reason to quit. Resilient people use failure as a **reason to work harder.**

- **J.K. Rowling** was rejected by 12 publishers before *Harry Potter* became a global success.

- **Walt Disney** was fired for "lacking imagination" before creating Disney.

- **Henry Ford** had five failed businesses before launching Ford Motor Company.

Every setback is a setup for a bigger comeback—if you refuse to quit.

5. Build a Strong Support System

Resilient people don't do it alone. They surround themselves with people who:
✓ Offer encouragement in tough times
✓ Challenge them to keep pushing forward
✓ Remind them of their strengths when they forget

If you don't have that support yet, **find it.** The right people will make you stronger.

Real-Life Story: Bouncing Back Stronger

Ava was a professional athlete with dreams of competing internationally. Just before her big tournament, she suffered a career-threatening injury.

Doctors told her she might never compete again. Most people would have given up. But Ava? **She chose resilience.**

✓ Instead of focusing on what she lost, she focused on what she could control—her recovery.
✓ She trained differently, worked on her mindset, and refused to quit.
✓ A year later, she returned to the competition and won.

When asked how she did it, she said:
"I refused to let failure define me. I used it to rebuild myself stronger."

Final Thought: Resilience is a Choice

✓ You can choose to see setbacks as the end—or as a stepping stone.
✓ You can choose to let failure break you—or make you better.
✓ You can choose to quit—or rise stronger than before.

You will win—not by avoiding struggles, but by proving that no struggle can stop you.

Next Chapter: The Power of Self-Belief

Now that you understand resilience, let's focus on **self-belief.** How do you develop unshakable confidence in yourself, even when others doubt you? Let's explore in the next chapter.

Chapter 14: The Power of Self-Belief

If you don't believe in yourself, why should anyone else?

Self-belief is the foundation of success. It's the difference between taking action and hesitating, between trying and giving up, between winning and staying stuck.

The truth is, **your belief in yourself shapes your reality.** If you believe you're capable, you'll find ways to succeed. If you believe you're not, you'll find excuses to fail.

Self-belief is not about arrogance—it's about **knowing your worth, trusting your abilities, and refusing to let doubt stop you.**

Why Self-Belief Matters

Every successful person, at some point, had to **believe in themselves before anyone else did.**

✓ **Self-belief pushes you to take action.**
✓ **Self-belief helps you overcome challenges.**
✓ **Self-belief allows you to ignore doubt and negativity.**
✓ **Self-belief gives you the courage to go after big goals.**

Without self-belief, even the best ideas and talents go to waste.

How Self-Doubt Destroys Success

✗ Self-doubt leads to hesitation. You question your abilities so much that you never take action.

✗ Self-doubt makes you settle. You don't go after big goals because you don't think you're good enough.

✗ Self-doubt makes you dependent on others for validation. Instead of trusting yourself, you wait for approval.

✗ Self-doubt makes you fear failure. You avoid risks because you don't trust that you can recover.

The longer you let self-doubt control you, the harder it becomes to break free.

How to Build Unshakable Self-Belief

1. Change Your Inner Dialogue

Your mind listens to what you tell it. If you constantly say, *"I'm not good enough,"* your brain will believe it.

Start replacing negative thoughts with powerful affirmations:

✗ *"I'm not ready."* → **✓** *"I am capable, and I will figure it out."*

✗ *"I don't have enough talent."* → **✓** *"Effort and consistency will take me where I want to go."*

✗ *"I always mess up."* → **✓** *"Every mistake is making me better."*

Repeat these statements daily. **Your words shape your confidence.**

2. Stop Waiting for Approval

If you need constant validation from others, **you'll never feel truly confident.**

✓ Winners don't wait for permission—they **trust their own judgment.**
✓ Winners don't need approval—they **know their worth.**

The only approval you need is **your own.**

3. Take Action, Even When You Don't Feel Ready

Many people wait for confidence **before** taking action—but confidence comes **after** action.

- You weren't confident riding a bike until you tried.

- You weren't confident driving a car until you practiced.

- You won't be confident in new challenges until you take the first step.

Action creates confidence. Start now, and the belief will follow.

4. Surround Yourself with Believers

Your environment influences your mindset. If you spend time with doubters and negative people, you will absorb their energy.

✓ **Find people who believe in you.**
✓ **Spend time with those who inspire you.**
✓ **Eliminate toxic voices that make you question yourself.**

If you can't find believers, **be your own biggest supporter.**

5. Keep Proof of Your Wins

Confidence grows when you recognize your own achievements.

✓ Keep a **"Victory Journal"** where you write down every success—big or small.
✓ Look back at past wins whenever doubt creeps in.
✓ Remind yourself: **You've succeeded before, and you will succeed again.**

Real-Life Story: From Doubt to Unshakable Confidence

Nathan was an aspiring artist, but for years, he never shared his work. Every time he thought about it, a voice in his head said:

- *"You're not talented enough."*

- *"People will criticize you."*

- *"You're not ready."*

One day, he decided to **ignore the doubt and post his art anyway.**

✓ The first post didn't go viral, but it gave him confidence.
✓ The second post got some positive feedback.
✓ The third post led to his first paid commission.

Today, Nathan is a full-time artist—not because he was the most talented, but because he **stopped doubting himself and started believing.**

Final Thought: Believe in Yourself First

✓ **If you don't believe in yourself, no one else will.**
✓ **If you don't trust yourself, you'll always play small.**
✓ **If you don't take action, you'll never know what's possible.**

You will win—but only when you start believing that you **deserve to.**

Next Chapter: Embracing Failure as a Teacher

Now that you've built self-belief, let's talk about **failure.** How can you stop fearing it and start using it as a stepping stone to success? Let's explore in the next chapter.

Chapter 15: Embracing Failure as a Teacher

Most people fear failure. They avoid risks, hesitate on big decisions, and play it safe—all because they don't want to fail.

But here's the truth: **Failure is not the opposite of success. It's part of success.**

Every person who has achieved greatness has failed— often **more times than they've succeeded.** The difference? **They didn't fear failure. They learned from it.**

If you want to win, **you must stop avoiding failure and start embracing it as a teacher.**

The Truth About Failure

Failure feels painful, embarrassing, and discouraging. But what most people don't realize is:

✓ **Failure gives you feedback.** Every mistake teaches you what works and what doesn't.
✓ **Failure builds resilience.** The more you fail and recover, the stronger you become.
✓ **Failure eliminates weak ideas.** If something doesn't work, it pushes you toward something better.
✓ **Failure is a test of commitment.** Many people quit when they fail. Winners keep going.

If you never fail, it means you're **not pushing yourself enough.**

How Winners Use Failure to Their Advantage

The world's most successful people failed—repeatedly. But they **used failure as a stepping stone.**

✓ **Albert Einstein** – Failed countless experiments before making scientific breakthroughs.

✓ **Oprah Winfrey** – Was fired from her first TV job before becoming a media powerhouse.

✓ **Steven Spielberg** – Rejected from film school multiple times before directing blockbusters.

✓ **Sara Blakely (Founder of Spanx)** – Failed in multiple careers before launching her billion-dollar brand.

These people didn't quit. **They failed, learned, adjusted, and tried again.**

Why Most People Fear Failure

✗ **They take failure personally** – Instead of seeing it as a learning process, they see it as proof they're not good enough.

✗ **They care too much about what others think** – They're afraid of looking bad or being judged.

✗ **They focus on short-term pain instead of long-term growth** – Failure hurts in the moment, but it leads to progress.

If you shift how you see failure, **you'll start to view it as a necessary step toward success.**

How to Embrace Failure and Keep Moving Forward

1. Redefine What Failure Means

Instead of seeing failure as a dead-end, start seeing it as **data.**

✗ **Old mindset:** *"I failed, so I'm not good enough."*
✓ **New mindset:** *"I failed, so I learned something valuable."*

Every failure contains information. **Ask yourself: What can I learn from this?**

2. Fail Fast, Fail Forward

Many people delay action because they fear failure. **But the longer you wait, the longer you delay success.**

✓ Take action quickly. If you fail, adjust and try again.
✓ The faster you fail, the faster you learn.
✓ The more you fail, the closer you get to success.

Failure is not the problem—**staying stuck is.**

3. Separate Your Identity from Your Failures

Just because you fail **at something** doesn't mean you **are a failure.**

✗ **Wrong belief:** *"I failed my business, so I'm a failure."*
✓ **Right belief:** *"My business failed, but I'm still capable of succeeding."*

Failure is an event, not a definition of who you are. **You always have the power to try again.**

4. Stop Caring About What Others Think

Many people fear failure because they're afraid of **looking bad.**

✓ But successful people **fail publicly and don't care.**
✓ They don't let the fear of judgment stop them from trying.

Remember: **People are too busy with their own lives to care about your failures. Keep moving.**

5. Keep a 'Lessons from Failure' Journal

Instead of avoiding failure, **document what you learn from it.**

✓ Write down every failure.
✓ Note the lessons from each experience.
✓ Use those lessons to improve next time.

Over time, you'll see that failure isn't something to fear—it's just **part of the process.**

Real-Life Story: Learning from Failure

Mia had always wanted to start a restaurant. When she finally opened one, things didn't go as planned—she miscalculated costs, struggled with marketing, and after two years, had to shut it down.

Most people would have given up. But Mia saw it differently.

✓ She **analyzed what went wrong.**
✓ She **learned better business strategies.**
✓ She **tried again—this time, with more knowledge.**

Her second restaurant was a success.

Mia didn't let failure define her. **She let it refine her.**

Final Thought: Failure is Your Greatest Teacher

✓ **If you fear failure, you'll never take risks.**
✓ **If you avoid failure, you'll never grow.**
✓ **If you embrace failure, you'll eventually succeed.**

You will win—but only if you stop fearing failure and start using it as fuel.

Next Chapter: The Science of Confidence – Building It Daily

Now that you've embraced failure, let's talk about **confidence.** How can you develop unshakable confidence every day? Let's find out in the next chapter.

Chapter 16: The Science of Confidence – Building It Daily

Confidence isn't something you're born with—it's something you build.

Some people assume confidence comes **after** success, but the truth is: **Confidence comes before success.** The more confident you are, the more action you take. The more action you take, the more success you create.

The good news? **Confidence is a skill**, and like any skill, it can be developed.

What is Confidence?

Confidence is **not** arrogance. It's not about thinking you're better than others.

✓ Confidence is trusting in your abilities and decisions.
✓ Confidence is taking action even when you're uncertain.
✓ Confidence is knowing you can handle whatever comes your way.

The strongest people aren't the ones who never doubt themselves—they're the ones who take action **despite** doubt.

The Science Behind Confidence

Confidence isn't just a feeling—it's a **neurological process.**

- Every time you take action, your brain builds **new neural pathways.**

- The more you practice something, the more natural it becomes.

- The less you hesitate, the more confident you feel.

In short: **Confidence is built through repetition and experience.**

Think about how you learned to ride a bike. At first, you were shaky and uncertain. But as you kept practicing, your brain adapted. Eventually, you stopped thinking about it—you just rode.

Confidence in **any** area of life works the same way.

How to Build Confidence Every Day

1. Take Action Before You Feel Ready

Many people think, *"I'll take action when I feel confident."* But that's backwards.

✓ Confidence comes **from taking action.**
✓ The more you act, the more your brain learns **you can handle it.**
✓ The first step is always the hardest—after that, momentum takes over.

✘ Waiting for confidence → Leads to inaction.
✓ Taking action → Builds confidence.

2. Use the 'Small Wins' Strategy

Confidence isn't built through huge achievements—it's built through **small, consistent wins.**

✓ If you fear public speaking, start by **speaking up in small meetings.**
✓ If you struggle with self-doubt, set **small daily challenges** and complete them.
✓ If you want to be more social, start by **talking to one new person a day.**

Each small win **tells your brain that you're capable.** Over time, these wins add up.

3. Change Your Body Language

Your posture and movements **affect how confident you feel.**

✓ Stand tall.
✓ Keep your shoulders back.
✓ Maintain eye contact.
✓ Speak with a steady voice.

Your brain takes cues from your body. **If you act confident, your brain follows.**

4. Stop Seeking Constant Approval

Many people lack confidence because they **rely on others for validation.**

✓ Confident people don't need permission to chase their dreams.
✓ Confident people don't let criticism stop them.
✓ Confident people trust their own judgment.

✗ If you live for approval, you'll **always** be controlled by others' opinions.

Trust yourself. **Your belief in yourself is what truly matters.**

5. Rewire Negative Self-Talk

Your inner dialogue **shapes your confidence.** If you constantly tell yourself, *"I'm not good enough,"* your brain will believe it.

Start replacing negative thoughts with empowering ones:

✗ *"I can't do this."* → ✓ *"I can figure this out."*
✗ *"I always mess up."* → ✓ *"I learn from every mistake."*
✗ *"I'm not talented enough."* → ✓ *"Effort and practice make me better."*

Your words matter. Choose them wisely.

6. Visualize Success

Top athletes, business leaders, and performers use **visualization** to build confidence.

✓ Close your eyes and picture yourself succeeding.
✓ Imagine yourself speaking confidently, winning a competition, or achieving your goal.
✓ Feel the emotions of success **before it happens.**

Your brain doesn't know the difference between real and imagined experiences. **The more you visualize success, the more natural confidence becomes.**

Real-Life Story: Building Confidence from Nothing

Daniel was terrified of speaking in public. His heart raced, his hands shook, and his mind went blank every time he had to talk in front of a group.

Instead of avoiding it forever, he decided to **train his confidence.**

✓ He started small—practicing in front of a mirror.
✓ He then spoke in front of close friends.
✓ Eventually, he joined a speaking club and improved with every attempt.

One year later, Daniel was giving presentations to large audiences.

His secret? **He didn't wait to feel confident—he acted until confidence became second nature.**

Final Thought: Confidence is Built, Not Born

√ **Confidence is a choice you make every day.**
√ **Confidence grows with action, not waiting.**
√ **Confidence is your greatest weapon against fear and self-doubt.**

You will win—but only if you **train your confidence like a muscle.**

Next Chapter: How to Stop Seeking Approval

Now that you've built confidence, let's talk about **approval-seeking.** Why do so many people depend on others' opinions, and how can you break free? Let's find out in the next chapter.

Chapter 17: How to Stop Seeking Approval

Too many people live their lives chasing one thing—**approval from others.**

- They hold back on their dreams because they fear judgment.

- They hesitate to speak up because they worry about what others will think.

- They shape their lives around fitting in instead of standing out.

But here's the truth: **The need for approval is a prison.** If you don't break free from it, you will never live life on your own terms.

The good news? **You don't need anyone's permission to be great.** The moment you stop seeking approval, you unlock a new level of confidence, freedom, and success.

Why We Crave Approval

Seeking approval isn't always a bad thing—it's part of human nature. From childhood, we are wired to seek validation because it gives us a sense of belonging.

But as we grow, this need can **become a weakness** if we let it control us.

✓ **Fear of Judgment** – You don't want people to think you're wrong, weird, or different.

✓ **Desire to Fit In** – Society teaches us to follow the crowd instead of standing out.

✓ **Low Self-Belief** – You trust others' opinions more than your own.

If you let approval-seeking run your life, you will:

✗ Make decisions based on what **others** want, not what **you** want.

✗ Hesitate to take risks, fearing criticism.

✗ Stay stuck in a comfort zone instead of chasing bold dreams.

The cost of approval-seeking is **your own happiness.**

Signs That You Seek Too Much Approval

Do any of these sound familiar?

✗ You overthink before posting on social media, afraid of what people will say.

✗ You say "yes" to things you don't want to do, just to please others.

✗ You hold back from sharing your ideas because you fear looking stupid.

✗ You change your decisions based on other people's opinions.

✗ You feel uncomfortable when someone disapproves of you.

If you relate to any of these, it's time to **reclaim your independence.**

How to Stop Seeking Approval and Take Control of Your Life

1. Realize That No One is Constantly Thinking About You

One of the biggest reasons people seek approval is because they think, *"Everyone is watching me."*

Here's the truth: **People are too busy with their own lives to care about yours.**

✓ They are worried about their own problems.
✓ They are thinking about themselves—not analyzing your every move.
✓ Even if they judge you, they will forget about it within minutes.

Once you accept this, **you'll stop caring so much about others' opinions.**

2. Build Strong Self-Trust

Approval-seeking happens when you **don't trust your own decisions.**

Instead of looking for validation, **start trusting yourself.**

✓ If you have a dream, **go for it—without waiting for permission.**

✓ If you believe in something, **stand by it—even if others disagree.**

✓ If you make a choice, **own it—without second-guessing.**

The more you trust yourself, the less you need approval from others.

3. Understand That Not Everyone Will Like You (And That's Okay)

No matter what you do, **some people will judge you.**

✓ Some people won't like your confidence.

✓ Some people will criticize your success.

✓ Some people will doubt your dreams.

And guess what? **That's THEIR problem, not yours.**

The most powerful people in the world have critics. If they worried about approval, they would have never changed history.

4. Stop Explaining Yourself

You don't need to justify every decision.

✗ **Wrong mindset:** *"I want to start my own business, but I need my family to understand why."*

✓ **Right mindset:** *"I want to start my own business, and I don't need anyone's permission."*

✗ **Wrong mindset:** *"I don't want to go to that party, but I need a good excuse."*
✓ **Right mindset:** *"I don't want to go—that's reason enough."*

Stop over-explaining. **Your choices don't need validation.**

5. Set Boundaries and Say "No" Without Guilt

People pleasers struggle to say no. But every time you say "yes" when you don't want to, **you give away control of your life.**

✓ Practice saying no—without over-apologizing.
✓ Stop explaining yourself when you decline something.
✓ Understand that **your time and energy are valuable.**

The right people will respect your boundaries. The wrong people? **Let them go.**

Real-Life Story: Breaking Free from Approval-Seeking

Emma always dreamed of becoming a writer, but she never pursued it.

- *"What if people think my writing is bad?"*

- *"What if my family doesn't support me?"*

- *"What if I embarrass myself?"*

For years, she let these thoughts hold her back. Then one day, she asked herself:

"Am I living for others, or am I living for myself?"

That question changed everything.

✓ She published her first book—even with doubts.
✓ She stopped caring about criticism and focused on **her passion.**
✓ She finally felt **free**—because she was no longer living for approval.

Today, Emma is a successful writer. **Not because she was fearless, but because she stopped letting fear control her.**

Final Thought: Stop Living for Others—Start Living for Yourself

✓ **You don't need permission to be great.**
✓ **Not everyone will like you—and that's okay.**
✓ **Your life is yours to live—stop letting approval-seeking hold you back.**

You will win—but only when you stop waiting for validation and start trusting yourself.

Next Chapter: Developing a Winning Mentality

Now that you've stopped seeking approval, it's time to fully step into a **winning mindset.** How do the most successful people think, and how can you adopt their mentality? Let's dive in next.

Chapter 18: Developing a Winning Mentality

Success isn't just about skill, luck, or talent—it's about **how you think.**

Some people rise to the top, not because they have special advantages, but because they **refuse to think like losers.** They develop a winning mentality—one that keeps them pushing forward no matter what.

The good news? **This mindset can be learned.** And once you train yourself to think like a winner, success in any area of life becomes inevitable.

What is a Winning Mentality?

A **winning mentality** is a mindset that pushes you to overcome obstacles, stay focused, and never settle for less than your full potential.

✓ **It's the belief that success is a choice.**
✓ **It's the discipline to do what others won't.**
✓ **It's the ability to keep going when others quit.**

How Winners Think Differently

✓ **Winners believe they are in control of their lives.**
✗ Losers believe life happens *to* them.

✓ **Winners focus on solutions.**

✗ Losers focus on problems.

✓ **Winners take responsibility.**

✗ Losers blame circumstances, people, or luck.

✓ **Winners stay consistent, even when they don't feel like it.**

✗ Losers only work when they're motivated.

✓ **Winners see setbacks as temporary.**

✗ Losers see setbacks as the end.

Success starts in the mind. If you think like a winner, you'll **act like one**—and eventually, you'll become one.

How to Develop a Winning Mentality

1. Take Full Responsibility for Your Life

The moment you blame others—your past, the economy, bad luck—you give away your power.

✓ Winners own their choices, their results, and their future.

✓ If something isn't working, they adjust instead of making excuses.

✓ They don't wait for circumstances to improve—they **create opportunities.**

Your life is in your hands. Act like it.

2. Set High Standards for Yourself

✓ Winners demand more from themselves than anyone else does.
✓ They don't settle for "good enough."
✓ They set goals that **stretch** them and force growth.

Ask yourself: *"Am I aiming high enough, or am I playing small?"*

If your goals don't scare you a little, **they're not big enough.**

3. Be Relentless in Taking Action

Motivation comes and goes. But winners don't rely on motivation—they rely on **discipline.**

✓ They take action even when they don't feel like it.
✓ They don't wait for the "perfect moment."
✓ They understand that **small, daily efforts create big results.**

You don't need to be the smartest or most talented—you just need to **outwork everyone else.**

4. Rewire How You See Failure

✗ **Losing mindset:** *"If I fail, I'm done."*
✓ **Winning mindset:** *"If I fail, I'll learn and try again."*

Every successful person has **failed more than others have even tried.**

✓ **Michael Jordan** missed over 9,000 shots but is considered the greatest basketball player of all time.
✓ **Arianna Huffington** was rejected by 36 publishers before her work became a global success.
✓ **Jeff Bezos** had multiple failed business ideas before launching Amazon.

The difference? **They didn't let failure stop them.**

5. Train Your Mind to Think Bigger

Most people stay stuck because their **vision is too small.** They aim for "just enough" instead of going after **greatness.**

✓ Winners think beyond their current circumstances.
✓ They don't settle for average when they know they can achieve more.
✓ They challenge themselves to dream bigger and take bold steps toward their goals.

What you believe is possible **becomes your reality.** So why not believe in something great?

6. Cut Out Weakness and Excuses

✓ Winners don't let **laziness, distractions, or negative influences** hold them back.
✓ They surround themselves with people who push them

to be better.
✓ They train themselves to be mentally strong—because winning starts in the mind.

If you want to win, **eliminate anything that weakens you.**

Real-Life Story: The Shift to a Winning Mindset

Liam was an average employee in a corporate job. He wanted more, but he kept telling himself:

- *"I'm not special."*

- *"Success is for other people."*

- *"I don't have the right skills."*

One day, he made a decision: **To think and act like a winner.**

✓ He started setting high goals instead of playing small.
✓ He stopped making excuses and took massive action.
✓ He invested in learning, built new skills, and **refused to quit.**

Today, Liam runs a multi-million-dollar business. The difference? **He trained his mind to expect success—and his actions followed.**

Final Thought: Winners Are Made, Not Born

✓ **Your mindset determines your success.**
✓ **Your actions shape your future.**

✓ **Your choices decide whether you win or stay stuck.**

You will win—but only when you **think, act, and push forward like a winner.**

Next Chapter: Why 'I Deserve It' Is the Wrong Approach

Now that you've developed a winning mentality, let's talk about **entitlement.** Why do so many people fail because they believe they "deserve" success? And how can you develop the right mindset instead? Let's find out in the next chapter.

Chapter 19: Why 'I Deserve It' Is the Wrong Approach

Many people believe that because they work hard, have good intentions, or have faced struggles, they **deserve** success.

- *"I've worked for years—I should be successful by now."*

- *"I'm a good person—I deserve happiness."*

- *"I put in effort—I deserve results."*

But here's the truth: **The world doesn't reward what you think you deserve. It rewards what you earn.**

This mindset shift is **critical** if you want to win.

The Problem with the 'I Deserve It' Mentality

When you believe you deserve something **just because**, you set yourself up for frustration.

✓ **Life doesn't owe you success.**
✓ **Hard work alone doesn't guarantee results—smart, consistent action does.**
✓ **You get what you fight for, not what you feel entitled to.**

Many people fail, not because they lack talent or opportunity, but because they **wait for success instead of creating it.**

Why This Mindset Holds You Back

✕ It Creates a Victim Mentality

When things don't go your way, you start blaming:

- *"I should have gotten that promotion."*

- *"It's unfair that I haven't succeeded yet."*

- *"Other people have it easier."*

Winners don't waste energy complaining. **They focus on solutions.**

✕ It Makes You Passive

People who believe they "deserve" success often **wait** for it instead of working relentlessly for it.

✓ They wait for the perfect moment.
✓ They wait for luck to favor them.
✓ They wait for someone to recognize their worth.

Winners don't wait. **They take control.**

✕ It Stops You from Adapting

When things don't go as expected, people with an entitlement mindset say:

- *"I worked hard—why didn't I get the results?"*

- *"This should have worked—I don't want to change my approach."*

113

But success isn't about **what you think should work**—it's about **what actually works.** Winners adjust, learn, and keep moving forward.

What to Do Instead: Earn It, Don't Expect It

1. Replace 'I Deserve' with 'I Will Create'

Instead of saying:
✗ *"I deserve success."*
Say:
✓ *"I will create success."*

Instead of saying:
✗ *"I deserve a better life."*
Say:
✓ *"I will build a better life."*

Shifting from **expecting to earning** changes everything.

2. Focus on Value, Not Just Effort

Many people think effort alone guarantees results. **It doesn't.**

✓ The market rewards value—not just hard work.
✓ People get opportunities because they solve problems, not because they "deserve" them.
✓ The key is to **provide more value**—to your business, your career, and the people around you.

Ask yourself: *"How can I make myself more valuable?"*

3. Take Extreme Ownership

Winners don't wait for the world to recognize them—they **take control.**

✓ If something isn't working, they **change their strategy.**
✓ If they don't get an opportunity, they **create one.**
✓ If they fail, they **own it, learn, and improve.**

Stop waiting for a break. **Be the person who makes things happen.**

4. Understand That Life is Not Fair—And That's Okay

Some people start with more advantages. That's reality.

✗ You can waste time complaining about it.
✓ Or you can **outwork, outlearn, and outlast everyone else.**

Many of the most successful people started with nothing—but they **didn't let that stop them.**

5. Adopt a 'Prove It' Mentality

Instead of saying, *"I should have success by now,"* ask yourself:

✓ *"Have I truly done everything possible to earn it?"*
✓ *"What more can I do to improve and grow?"*
✓ *"How can I prove to myself and the world that I'm worth it?"*

The world doesn't care what you think you deserve. **It cares about what you deliver.**

Real-Life Story: From Entitlement to Achievement

Noah was a talented musician. He spent years practicing, but his career wasn't taking off.

- *"I work hard—I deserve to be successful."*

- *"Other artists aren't as talented as me, but they're more famous."*

- *"It's unfair that I haven't made it yet."*

Then one day, he realized: **Success wasn't about what he felt he deserved—it was about what he created.**

✓ He stopped waiting and started networking.
✓ He studied marketing instead of just music.
✓ He put out content daily, not just when he felt like it.

Within a year, he had a growing fan base and landed major gigs.

What changed? **His mindset.**

Final Thought: Stop Expecting—Start Earning

✓ **Success is not given. It's taken.**
✓ **The world doesn't reward effort—it rewards results.**
✓ **You don't deserve success. You create it.**

You will win—but only when you stop waiting and start making it happen.

Next Chapter: Self-Discipline – The Ultimate Key to Success

Now that you understand why entitlement is dangerous, let's talk about **self-discipline.** How can you train yourself to stay consistent, focused, and unstoppable? Let's find out in the next chapter.

Chapter 20: Self-Discipline – The Ultimate Key to Success

Motivation comes and goes. Willpower fades. But **self-discipline?** That's what separates winners from everyone else.

Self-discipline is the ability to **do what needs to be done, even when you don't feel like doing it.** It's waking up early when you'd rather sleep in. It's choosing work over distractions. It's staying consistent when others give up.

The truth? **Success isn't about talent or luck—it's about discipline.**

Why Self-Discipline Matters More Than Motivation

Many people rely on **motivation** to get things done. But motivation is **temporary**—it's easy to feel inspired today and lazy tomorrow.

✓ Motivation is emotional—it depends on how you feel.
✓ Discipline is a habit—it gets done regardless of feelings.

The most successful people in the world don't **always** feel like working hard. They just do it **anyway.**

The Cost of a Lack of Discipline

If you lack self-discipline:
✘ You set goals but never follow through.
✘ You start projects but never finish them.
✘ You get distracted by comfort instead of pushing yourself.
✘ You stay stuck in the same place, year after year.

But when you **train yourself to be disciplined,** everything changes.

✓ You become **consistent.**
✓ You take action, even on hard days.
✓ You develop habits that push you forward.

Discipline is the **shortcut to success**—because **while others quit, you keep going.**

How to Build Unshakable Self-Discipline

1. Set Clear, Non-Negotiable Standards

Winners don't just set goals—they set **rules** for themselves.

Instead of saying:
✘ *"I'll try to wake up early."*
Say:
✓ *"I wake up at 5 AM every day, no excuses."*

Instead of saying:
✘ *"I'll go to the gym when I have time."*
Say:

✓ *"I train every Monday, Wednesday, and Friday—no exceptions."*

When something becomes **non-negotiable,** you stop making excuses.

2. Create a Daily Routine and Stick to It

Discipline isn't about willpower—it's about **habits.**

✓ **Wake up and sleep at the same time every day.**
✓ **Schedule work, exercise, and learning like appointments.**
✓ **Follow the same morning and evening routine.**

The more structured your life is, the less you rely on motivation.

3. Stop Negotiating with Yourself

Many people fail because they give themselves an **easy way out.**

- *"I don't feel like working today—I'll do it tomorrow."*
- *"One more episode won't hurt."*
- *"Skipping one day won't matter."*

✗ **These small decisions destroy your progress.**

✓ Winners don't argue with themselves. **They follow through, no matter what.**

The rule is simple: **Don't think. Just do.**

4. Remove Distractions and Weaknesses

Your environment either **supports discipline** or **destroys it.**

✓ If your phone distracts you, **put it in another room while you work.**
✓ If junk food tempts you, **don't keep it in the house.**
✓ If social media wastes time, **set limits or delete apps.**

Discipline isn't just about willpower—it's about **removing temptations** so success becomes automatic.

5. Train Yourself to Do Hard Things Daily

The more comfortable you are with **difficulty,** the stronger your discipline becomes.

✓ Take cold showers.
✓ Work out even when you don't feel like it.
✓ Read and learn every day—even when it's boring.
✓ Wake up early—even when you'd rather sleep in.

Each time you **choose discomfort,** you train your brain to **stop taking the easy way out.**

Real-Life Story: How Discipline Changed Everything

Ethan wanted to become a professional athlete, but he struggled with consistency.

- He trained only when he felt motivated.
- He skipped workouts when he was tired.
- He didn't follow a strict diet.

One day, he realized: **Talent wasn't enough. He needed discipline.**

✓ He created a strict daily schedule.
✓ He followed his training plan **no matter what.**
✓ He eliminated distractions and made success **non-negotiable.**

A year later, he was in the best shape of his life—and competing at the highest level.

His secret? Discipline, not motivation.

Final Thought: Discipline = Freedom

✓ **If you master discipline, you master life.**
✓ **If you develop discipline, success becomes inevitable.**
✓ **If you stay disciplined, you will win.**

You will win—but only if you **stay consistent, no matter what.**

Next Chapter: Small Steps, Big Results

Now that you understand discipline, let's talk about **small actions that lead to massive success.** How can tiny daily habits transform your life? Let's explore in the next chapter.

Section 3:

Taking Actions

Chapter 21: Small Steps, Big Results

Most people believe success comes from **one big breakthrough.** They think they need a perfect moment, a life-changing opportunity, or a massive stroke of luck.

But the truth? **Success is built on small, consistent actions.**

Every major achievement—whether in business, health, or personal growth—comes from **tiny daily habits** repeated over time.

✓ **A book is written one page at a time.**
✓ **A business is built one customer at a time.**
✓ **A healthy body is created one workout at a time.**

The secret to winning? **Small steps, taken consistently, lead to massive results.**

Why Small Steps Matter More Than Big Ones

Big goals can feel **overwhelming.** This is why most people never start.

✓ If you focus on losing 20 kg, it feels impossible.
✓ If you focus on writing a book, it feels like too much work.
✓ If you focus on building a million-dollar business, it feels unrealistic.

But what if, instead of thinking big, you thought **small**?

- **Instead of losing 20 kg, focus on one healthy meal per day.**
- **Instead of writing a book, focus on one paragraph per day.**
- **Instead of building a business, focus on one customer at a time.**

Suddenly, everything feels manageable. **And when small efforts compound over time, success is inevitable.**

The Power of the 1% Improvement Rule

If you improve by just **1% every day,** you will be **37 times better** in a year.

✓ 1% might seem like nothing today, but over time, it **transforms everything.**
✓ Small, consistent improvements **outperform big, unsustainable changes.**
✓ Success is a game of **consistency, not intensity.**

Ask yourself: *What's one small thing I can do today to improve?*

How to Apply Small Steps for Big Success

1. Break Big Goals into Tiny Actions

Instead of setting massive goals that overwhelm you, **focus on daily actions.**

✓ **Want to get fit?** Do just 10 minutes of exercise daily.
✓ **Want to start a business?** Work on it for 30

minutes every evening.
✓ **Want to save money?** Set aside just $5 per day.

The **smaller** the action, the **easier** it is to start—and the **faster** you build momentum.

2. Focus on Consistency, Not Perfection

The key to progress is **showing up daily, even when you don't feel like it.**

✗ Don't aim for **perfection.**
✓ Aim for **consistency.**

- **A short workout is better than no workout.**
- **Writing one page is better than waiting for inspiration.**
- **Taking small action today is better than waiting for the perfect moment.**

Perfection is the enemy of progress. **Consistency wins every time.**

3. Track Your Progress

✓ Winners measure their actions.
✓ Tracking keeps you motivated.
✓ Seeing progress, even in small ways, keeps you moving forward.

Try using:
▦ **A habit tracker** to check off daily progress.

📖 **A journal** to reflect on small wins.
📈 **A progress chart** to see long-term growth.

Every small victory **proves you're getting closer to success.**

4. Trust the Process—Results Will Follow

Success doesn't happen overnight. **It happens gradually.**

Think about:

- **Bamboo trees** take years to grow underground before they shoot up rapidly.
- **Muscles don't grow overnight**—they develop with consistent effort.
- **Businesses take years to become successful**— but every small action builds toward that.

Be patient. Stay consistent. The results will come.

Real-Life Story: The Power of Small Steps

Lucas wanted to become fluent in Spanish, but he kept procrastinating. He thought he needed hours of study daily.

Then he changed his approach:

✓ He studied **just 10 minutes a day.**
✓ He listened to **one Spanish podcast per day.**
✓ He practiced speaking **one sentence per day.**

After a year, Lucas was holding full conversations—**all from small, daily actions.**

Final Thought: Small Steps, Big Impact

✓ **Success isn't about giant leaps—it's about small, consistent actions.**
✓ **Improving just 1% every day leads to massive results over time.**
✓ **If you start small and stay consistent, success is inevitable.**

You will win—but only if you **commit to small steps every day.**

Next Chapter: The 5-Second Rule – Overcoming Hesitation

Now that you understand the power of small steps, let's talk about **how to take action instantly.** What if you could break hesitation and start immediately? Let's explore the 5-Second Rule in the next chapter.

Chapter 22: The 5-Second Rule – Overcoming Hesitation

How many times have you had a great idea, a goal, or an opportunity—but instead of taking action, you hesitated?

You thought about starting a business, speaking up in a meeting, or going to the gym. But instead of moving forward, you **paused.** And in that moment of hesitation, doubt crept in.

"What if I fail?"
"What if I'm not ready?"
"Maybe I'll do it later."

And just like that, **the moment passed, and you did nothing.**

This is why most people stay stuck. They overthink, hesitate, and let fear stop them.

But what if you could break this pattern instantly?

That's where **The 5-Second Rule** comes in.

What is The 5-Second Rule?

Created by **Mel Robbins**, the 5-Second Rule is a simple but powerful technique:

✓ The moment you have an instinct to act on a goal, **count backward—5, 4, 3, 2, 1—then move.**
✓ By taking action within **five seconds**, you shut down fear, overthinking, and hesitation.

✓ You override doubt and **train your brain to act immediately.**

This rule works because **your brain is wired to stop you from taking risks.** If you hesitate for too long, your mind will talk you out of it.

The secret? Act before your brain has a chance to stop you.

Why The 5-Second Rule Works

✓ **It stops overthinking.** The more you think, the less likely you are to act. The 5-Second Rule forces immediate action.
✓ **It rewires your brain for confidence.** When you act quickly, you train yourself to be bold and decisive.
✓ **It builds momentum.** Taking one small action leads to another, and before you know it, you're making massive progress.

The longer you wait, the harder it becomes. **The faster you act, the easier it gets.**

How to Use The 5-Second Rule in Real Life

1. Overcome Procrastination

✗ **Before:** *"I'll start later."*
✓ **Now:** *"5-4-3-2-1... Start now."*

- Need to go to the gym? **5-4-3-2-1—get up and put on your shoes.**

- Have work to do? **5-4-3-2-1—open your laptop and start.**
- Want to wake up early? **5-4-3-2-1—get out of bed immediately.**

Every time you hesitate, **count down and take action.**

2. Stop Fear from Holding You Back

Fear of failure, rejection, or embarrassment stops people from taking chances.

✗ **Before:** *"What if I embarrass myself?"*
✓ **Now:** *"5-4-3-2-1—Go for it."*

- Want to speak up in a meeting? **5-4-3-2-1—Raise your hand.**
- Want to introduce yourself to someone new? **5-4-3-2-1—Say hello.**
- Want to post your content online? **5-4-3-2-1—Hit publish.**

You don't have to feel ready—you just have to act.

3. Build Self-Discipline

Discipline isn't about willpower—it's about **making quick decisions and following through.**

✓ **When you don't feel like working, count down and start anyway.**
✓ **When you're tempted by distractions, count down and refocus.**

✓ **When you feel lazy, count down and do one productive thing.**

Discipline is built by taking action **immediately, not later.**

Real-Life Story: How The 5-Second Rule Changed Everything

Mark always struggled with self-doubt. He wanted to apply for a promotion, but every time he thought about it, fear held him back.

- *"What if I'm not good enough?"*
- *"What if they reject me?"*
- *"Maybe I should wait."*

Then, he discovered **The 5-Second Rule.**

✓ The next time he saw the job opening, he **counted down—5-4-3-2-1—submitted his application.**
✓ The next time he wanted to speak in a meeting, he **counted down and raised his hand.**
✓ The next time he felt nervous, he **used the rule and took action anyway.**

A few months later, he got the promotion. Not because he was the most skilled—**but because he stopped hesitating and started acting.**

Final Thought: Action is the Antidote to Fear

✓ **Overthinking keeps you stuck—immediate action sets you free.**

√ **Hesitation kills confidence—quick decisions build it.**
√ **You don't need to feel ready—you just need to act.**

You will win—but only if you **stop hesitating and start moving.**

5-4-3-2-1—GO.

Next Chapter: Creating Systems, Not Just Goals

Now that you know how to take action instantly, let's talk about **why systems are more powerful than goals.** How can you set up habits that make success inevitable? Let's find out in the next chapter.

Chapter 23: Creating Systems, Not Just Goals

Most people set goals. Few people achieve them.

Why?

Because **goals alone don't create success—systems do.**

A goal is **what you want.**
A system is **how you get there.**

The secret to winning? **Stop focusing only on goals and start building systems that make success automatic.**

Why Goals Aren't Enough

Most people think setting a goal is the key to success. But here's why goals alone don't work:

✘ **Goals rely on motivation.** You might feel excited when setting a goal, but that feeling fades.
✘ **Goals have a finish line.** Once you reach the goal, you may stop progressing.
✘ **Goals don't change your habits.** You need a system to keep making progress long-term.

Example:

- A goal is **"I want to lose 10 kg."**
- A system is **"I will eat healthy meals and exercise for 30 minutes daily."**

A system makes success inevitable—even when motivation is low.

What's the Difference Between a Goal and a System?

✓ A goal is the destination. A system is the path.
✓ A goal is temporary. A system creates lasting success.
✓ A goal is about results. A system is about daily actions.

If you focus only on the goal, you may feel lost. **But if you focus on the system, progress becomes automatic.**

How to Build Systems for Success

1. Focus on Daily Actions, Not Just the End Result

Instead of setting goals like:
✗ *"I want to write a book."*
Say:
✓ *"I will write 500 words every day."*

Instead of:
✗ *"I want to save $10,000."*
Say:
✓ *"I will save $10 every day."*

Tiny actions, done consistently, lead to massive results.

2. Make It a Habit

Success is not about **willpower**—it's about **habits.**

✓ Winners don't rely on motivation. They **make winning a habit.**
✓ They **schedule their success** so it happens automatically.
✓ They remove distractions, so their system runs smoothly.

Example: If you want to exercise daily:
✓ Set your gym clothes out the night before.
✓ Schedule workouts at the same time every day.
✓ Make it part of your routine—just like brushing your teeth.

The easier you make your system, the harder it becomes to fail.

3. Track Your Progress

✓ Measure your daily actions, not just the final outcome.
✓ Keep a **habit tracker** to mark every small win.
✓ Celebrate consistency—even when progress feels slow.

Success isn't about big wins—it's about **showing up every day.**

4. Design Your Environment for Success

Your surroundings influence your actions. **Make success easier by setting up the right environment.**

✓ If you want to eat healthier, **keep junk food out of the house.**
✓ If you want to read more, **place books where you'll see them.**
✓ If you want to stay focused, **turn off notifications and clear distractions.**

The less effort it takes to follow your system, **the more likely you are to stick to it.**

Real-Life Story: How Systems Beat Goals

Sophie wanted to become a marathon runner, but every time she set a goal, she failed.

- She'd train for a few weeks, then quit.
- She relied on motivation, which faded quickly.
- She kept restarting but never finished.

Then she changed her approach.

✓ Instead of setting a **goal**, she built a **system.**
✓ She committed to **running 3 km every morning— no excuses.**
✓ She tracked her runs and made it a **daily habit.**

Months later, she didn't just run a marathon—**she kept running daily, long after the race.**

Why? **Because she built a system that made running part of her life.**

Final Thought: Systems Create Lasting Success

✓ **Goals give direction, but systems create progress.**
✓ **Small daily actions matter more than big plans.**
✓ **If you focus on your system, success will take care of itself.**

You will win—but only if you **build systems that make winning inevitable.**

Next Chapter: Time Management for Peak Performance

Now that you know how to build systems, let's talk about **how to manage your time effectively.** How can you maximize productivity without burning out? Let's find out in the next chapter.

Chapter 24: Time Management for Peak Performance

Time is the most valuable resource you have. You can lose money and earn it back, but **once time is gone, it's gone forever.**

Yet, most people waste time on distractions, procrastination, and low-value tasks. Winners? **They treat time like gold.**

If you want to achieve more in less time, you must learn how to **manage your time like a high performer.**

Why Time Management is the Key to Success

✓ **You get more done in less time.** High performers work smarter, not just harder.
✓ **You eliminate stress.** When you manage time well, you avoid last-minute panic.
✓ **You create space for what truly matters.** Instead of feeling "busy," you focus on impact.
✓ **You achieve your goals faster.** Small, consistent effort leads to massive results.

The problem? **Most people don't control their time—time controls them.**

The Biggest Time Wasters

Before we fix time management, let's identify the biggest problems:

✗ **Procrastination** – You wait for the "perfect moment" instead of starting now.
✗ **Distractions** – Endless scrolling, notifications, and interruptions destroy focus.
✗ **Multitasking** – Doing too many things at once lowers efficiency and quality.
✗ **Lack of Prioritization** – You waste time on low-value tasks instead of what truly matters.

The solution? Take control of your time with proven strategies.

How to Master Time Management

1. The 80/20 Rule – Focus on High-Impact Tasks

Not all tasks are equal. The **80/20 Rule** (Pareto Principle) states:

✓ **80% of your results come from 20% of your actions.**
✓ The key to success is **identifying and focusing on that 20%.**

Ask yourself:
☞ *"What few tasks create the biggest results?"*
☞ *"What can I eliminate or delegate?"*

Work smarter, not just harder.

2. The Time-Blocking Method

Instead of working randomly, **schedule specific time blocks** for deep work.

✓ Assign each task a fixed time.
✓ Remove distractions and focus only on that task.
✓ Treat time blocks like important meetings—**non-negotiable.**

Example:
🕘 **9:00–11:00 AM** – High-priority work
🕐 **12:00–12:30 PM** – Lunch break
🕐 **2:00–3:00 PM** – Meetings/calls
⏰ **5:00–6:00 PM** – Exercise

When you control your schedule, **you control your results.**

3. The 2-Minute Rule – Beat Procrastination Instantly

If a task takes **less than 2 minutes, do it immediately.**

✓ Reply to that quick email.
✓ Organize your desk.
✓ Take the first small step toward a big task.

This eliminates small tasks **before they pile up** and removes excuses.

4. The Pomodoro Technique – Stay Focused

Use the **Pomodoro Technique** to maximize focus:

✓ **Work for 25 minutes** (fully focused).
✓ **Take a 5-minute break.**
✓ Repeat 4 times, then take a **longer break (15–30 min).**

This prevents burnout and keeps your brain sharp.

5. Learn to Say "No"

Your time is **limited.** If you say yes to everything, you'll never have time for what matters.

✓ Say no to unimportant meetings.
✓ Say no to distractions.
✓ Say no to tasks that don't align with your goals.

Every **"yes"** should be a **HELL YES.** If it's not, **it's a no.**

Real-Life Story: How Time Management Transformed Productivity

Megan was constantly overwhelmed. She worked long hours but never seemed to get ahead.

Then, she changed her approach:

✓ She used the **80/20 Rule** to focus only on high-value tasks.

✓ She **blocked time** for deep work and eliminated distractions.

✓ She used the **Pomodoro Technique** to stay focused.

Within months, Megan got more done in **less time.** Her stress disappeared, and she finally had time for herself.

The difference? She managed her time like a winner.

Final Thought: Time is Your Greatest Asset

✓ **Winners control their time—losers let time control them.**

✓ **Focus on what truly matters, and eliminate everything else.**

✓ **Master time, and you will master success.**

You will win—but only if you **treat your time like the valuable asset it is.**

Next Chapter: Breaking Bad Habits, Building Better Ones

Now that you know how to manage time effectively, let's talk about **habits.** How can you eliminate bad habits and build powerful ones that lead to success? Let's find out in the next chapter.

Chapter 25: Breaking Bad Habits, Building Better Ones

Your habits shape your life.

✓ **Good habits** lead to success, health, and happiness.
✗ **Bad habits** keep you stuck, frustrated, and unfulfilled.

The difference between winners and everyone else? **Winners design their habits intentionally.**

The secret to success isn't about working harder—it's about **replacing bad habits with good ones that make winning automatic.**

Why Habits Matter More Than Motivation

Motivation is **temporary.** It fades.

Habits are **automatic.** They stick.

✓ **You don't think about brushing your teeth—you just do it.**
✓ **You don't decide daily whether to drink coffee—it's a habit.**
✓ **If you create good habits, success becomes effortless.**

The goal? **Make good habits easy and bad habits hard.**

How Bad Habits Keep You Stuck

Bad habits drain time, energy, and focus.

✘ Checking social media first thing in the morning = Distracted, unproductive day.
✘ Skipping workouts = Weak body, low energy.
✘ Procrastinating = Dreams delayed, goals missed.
✘ Complaining = Negative mindset, no progress.

If you want to change your life, start by changing your habits.

How to Break Bad Habits

1. Identify the Habit Loop

Every habit follows a **loop**:

☞ **Trigger** – What starts the habit? (Example: Stress)
☞ **Action** – The habit itself. (Example: Eating junk food)
☞ **Reward** – What you get from it. (Example: Temporary comfort)

To break a bad habit, **replace the action with something better.**

Example:
✘ Old habit: Stress → Eat junk food → Feel temporary relief.
✓ New habit: Stress → Take a 5-minute walk → Feel refreshed.

You don't eliminate bad habits—you replace them.

2. Remove Temptation

If you struggle with a bad habit, **make it harder to do.**

✓ Want to stop checking your phone? **Put it in another room.**
✓ Want to stop eating junk food? **Don't keep it in the house.**
✓ Want to stop wasting time? **Block distracting websites.**

Out of sight, out of mind.

3. Make It Inconvenient

The harder a bad habit is, the less likely you'll do it.

✓ **Log out of social media** so it takes effort to log in.
✓ **Put your remote far away** so watching TV is less convenient.
✓ **Unsubscribe from shopping emails** so you're not tempted to buy.

Make bad habits a hassle, and they'll disappear.

How to Build Better Habits

1. Start Small (The 2-Minute Rule)

If a habit feels too big, **shrink it.**

✓ **Want to read more?** Read one page a day.
✓ **Want to exercise?** Do five push-ups.
✓ **Want to write?** Write one sentence.

The hardest part of any habit is **starting.** Make it easy.

2. Use Habit Stacking

Tie a new habit to an existing one.

✓ **After I brush my teeth, I will drink a glass of water.**
✓ **After I drink coffee, I will write my goals.**
✓ **After I finish work, I will go for a walk.**

Stacking habits makes them automatic.

3. Track and Reward Progress

✓ **Use a habit tracker** to check off daily wins.
✓ **Set small rewards** to stay motivated.
✓ **Celebrate progress, not perfection.**

Example: **If you work out 5 days in a row, treat yourself to a movie.**

Small rewards keep habits fun and sustainable.

Real-Life Story: The Power of Tiny Habits

David struggled with his health. He tried intense workout plans but quit after a few weeks.

Then he changed his approach:

✓ Instead of **one-hour workouts,** he started with **5 minutes daily.**
✓ Instead of **cutting all junk food,** he replaced one unhealthy meal per day.
✓ Instead of **big changes,** he focused on **small, consistent steps.**

Months later, he was in the best shape of his life—**not because he worked harder, but because he built better habits.**

Final Thought: Habits Shape Your Future

✓ **Your life is a reflection of your daily habits.**
✓ **Break bad habits, replace them with good ones.**
✓ **Small changes, repeated daily, lead to massive results.**

You will win—but only if you **master your habits.**

Next Chapter: The 1% Improvement Rule

Now that you understand habits, let's talk about **how small improvements can lead to unstoppable success.** Let's dive in next!

Chapter 26: The 1% Improvement Rule

Most people believe success happens overnight. They think they need a massive breakthrough, a perfect plan, or a sudden burst of motivation.

But the truth? **Real success comes from improving just 1% every day.**

✓ **1% better today = 37 times better in a year.**
✓ **Tiny improvements, repeated daily, lead to massive results.**
✓ **Winning isn't about giant leaps—it's about small, consistent progress.**

If you want long-term success, **stop looking for shortcuts and start focusing on daily improvements.**

The Power of the 1% Rule

If you improve just **1% every day**, you don't just get 365% better in a year—you get **3,778% better** due to compounding.

Why? Because **small improvements build on each other.**

Example:

- **A writer** who writes just 200 words per day will have a full book in a year.

- **A runner** who runs 1% further each time will be a marathoner in months.
- **A business owner** who improves customer service by 1% daily will dominate the market.

Tiny gains lead to unstoppable momentum.

Why Most People Fail at Improvement

✗ **They expect instant results.** When they don't see progress fast, they quit.
✗ **They focus on big changes.** They think success requires massive effort instead of small, daily actions.
✗ **They lack patience.** They underestimate how powerful small improvements become over time.

Success isn't about working harder—it's about **getting a little better every single day.**

How to Apply the 1% Rule in Your Life

1. Focus on Small Wins Daily

Instead of trying to **change everything overnight**, focus on one small improvement at a time.

✓ **Want to get healthier?** Add one extra glass of water today.
✓ **Want to learn a skill?** Study for just 10 minutes daily.
✓ **Want to be more productive?** Reduce one distraction from your day.

Small wins **build confidence and momentum.**

2. Track Progress, No Matter How Small

✓ Keep a **journal** of daily improvements.
✓ Use a **habit tracker** to check off small wins.
✓ Review progress weekly to see how far you've come.

Tracking makes progress **visible and motivating.**

3. Apply 'Tiny Tweaks' Instead of Drastic Changes

✓ **In fitness:** Do 1% more reps or run 1% longer.
✓ **In business:** Improve customer service by just 1% each day.
✓ **In learning:** Read one extra page per day.

Over time, these tiny improvements turn into **huge success.**

4. Stay Consistent – Even When Progress Feels Slow

The 1% Rule works **only if you stick with it.**

✓ Winners show up daily—even when they don't feel like it.
✓ Progress might feel slow at first, but **it compounds over time.**

✓ The hardest part is starting—**momentum will take care of the rest.**

Remember: **Small progress daily > Big effort once in a while.**

Real-Life Story: The Power of Small Improvements

Emily struggled with public speaking. She used to freeze in front of an audience.

Instead of trying to **become a great speaker overnight**, she used the **1% Rule:**

✓ She practiced speaking for **just 5 minutes a day.**
✓ She challenged herself to **speak in small groups before big audiences.**
✓ She recorded herself and **improved 1% each time.**

A year later, she gave a TEDx talk—**all because of tiny, daily improvements.**

Final Thought: Small Steps = Big Wins

✓ **1% daily improvements lead to massive success over time.**
✓ **Slow progress is still progress.**
✓ **If you stay consistent, success is inevitable.**

You will win—but only if you **commit to improving just 1% every day.**

Next Chapter: How to Take Control of Your Emotions

Now that you understand small improvements, let's talk about **emotional mastery.** How can you stay focused, motivated, and in control—even when life gets tough? Let's explore in the next chapter.

Chapter 27: How to Take Control of Your Emotions

Your emotions can either be your **greatest strength or your biggest weakness.**

✓ If you control your emotions, you stay focused, make smart decisions, and keep moving forward.
✗ If your emotions control you, you react impulsively, lose focus, and sabotage your progress.

Winners **don't let emotions dictate their actions.** They train themselves to stay calm, focused, and in control—**no matter what.**

The good news? **Emotional control is a skill, and you can develop it.**

Why Most People Struggle with Emotions

Most people let emotions **control them** because they:

✗ **React instead of responding.** They act on impulse instead of thinking first.
✗ **Let fear and doubt take over.** They allow emotions to stop them from taking action.
✗ **Let small setbacks ruin their day.** They let temporary problems affect long-term success.

But here's the truth: **Emotions are temporary. If you learn to manage them, you gain power over your life.**

How to Take Control of Your Emotions

1. Pause Before You React

Emotions make you act **without thinking.**

✓ Instead of **reacting immediately, take a deep breath.**
✓ Give yourself **five seconds** before responding to situations.
✓ Ask yourself: *"Is this emotion helping me or hurting me?"*

A few seconds of pause **can prevent regretful decisions.**

2. Separate Emotion from Action

You don't have to **act** on every emotion.

✗ **Feeling angry?** Don't send that impulsive message.
✗ **Feeling demotivated?** Show up anyway—discipline matters more.
✗ **Feeling frustrated?** Step away, clear your mind, then decide.

Winners act based on logic, not just feelings.

3. Train Your Mind to Handle Stress

✓ **Use breathing techniques.** Slow, deep breaths calm your nervous system.
✓ **Practice mindfulness.** Stay present instead of

155

drowning in negative thoughts.

✓ **Adopt the 'No Reaction' mindset.** The less you react, the more control you have.

Your ability to handle stress = **Your ability to succeed.**

4. Control Negative Self-Talk

The way you talk to yourself affects your emotions.

✗ *"I always mess up."* → ✓ *"I learn and improve."*
✗ *"I'm not good enough."* → ✓ *"I can develop this skill."*
✗ *"This is too hard."* → ✓ *"I can figure this out."*

Change your words, and you'll change how you feel.

5. Focus on What You Can Control

You can't control **everything**—but you can control **how you respond.**

✓ **Traffic made you late?** Getting angry won't fix it—stay calm.
✓ **Someone criticized you?** Don't waste energy—use it as feedback.
✓ **Unexpected failure?** Learn from it and move on.

When you focus on what you **can** control, emotions lose their power over you.

Real-Life Story: The Power of Emotional Control

Chris used to let emotions ruin his productivity. If he felt demotivated, he skipped work. If he got negative feedback, he doubted himself for days.

One day, he decided to change.

✓ He practiced **pausing before reacting.**
✓ He separated **emotion from action.**
✓ He focused only on **what he could control.**

A year later, he was more successful, more confident, and no longer controlled by emotions.

Final Thought: Master Your Emotions, Master Your Life

✓ **Emotions are temporary—don't let them control your actions.**
✓ **You can't control everything, but you can control how you respond.**
✓ **The more control you have over your emotions, the more unstoppable you become.**

You will win—but only if you **stay calm, stay focused, and stay in control.**

Next Chapter: The Magic of Consistency

Now that you've mastered your emotions, let's talk about **consistency.** How can you stay committed to your goals, even when progress feels slow? Let's find out in the next chapter.

Chapter 28: The Magic of Consistency

If you want to know the secret to success, it's this: **Consistency beats talent, luck, and motivation.**

✓ **Anyone can start something.** Few people keep going.
✓ **Anyone can work hard for a day.** Few people work hard every day.
✓ **Anyone can be motivated.** Few people stay disciplined when motivation fades.

The most successful people in the world? **They mastered the power of consistency.**

If you can stay consistent—**even when progress feels slow, even when results aren't immediate—you will win.**

Why Consistency is the Key to Everything

Most people fail **not because they're not capable,** but because they're **not consistent.**

✗ They go to the gym for a week, then quit.
✗ They work on their goals for a month, then lose focus.
✗ They start strong but don't follow through.

But winners? **They show up every day, no matter what.**

✓ **A writer who writes daily will finish a book.**
✓ **A business owner who improves daily will**

build an empire.
✓ An athlete who trains daily will become unstoppable.

Success isn't about big efforts once in a while. **It's about small efforts, repeated daily.**

The Biggest Myths About Consistency

✗ "I need motivation to be consistent."
✓ Truth: Motivation is temporary—discipline keeps you going.

✗ "I have to make huge progress every day."
✓ Truth: Even small progress adds up over time.

✗ "If I miss a day, I've failed."
✓ Truth: One bad day doesn't matter—what matters is bouncing back.

Consistency is **not about perfection.** It's about showing up more often than not.

How to Stay Consistent (Even When You Don't Feel Like It)

1. Make It Too Easy to Fail

The simpler your routine, **the easier it is to stay consistent.**

✓ **Want to exercise?** Do just 5 minutes a day.
✓ **Want to write?** Write one sentence daily.
✓ **Want to learn?** Read one page every day.

Once you start, **momentum takes over.**

2. Use 'Never Miss Twice' Rule

Missing one day? **No problem.**
Missing two days? **That's how failure starts.**

✓ If you skip a workout today, **get back to it tomorrow.**
✓ If you miss a study session, **make sure you show up next time.**

Success is built by **getting back on track quickly.**

3. Track Your Progress

✓ Keep a habit tracker to see your streaks.
✓ Mark an 'X' on your calendar every time you follow through.
✓ The longer your streak, the harder it becomes to break.

Seeing your progress **keeps you accountable.**

4. Make It a Non-Negotiable Habit

✗ **Don't rely on willpower.**
✓ **Make success automatic.**

✓ **Schedule workouts like meetings.**
✓ **Set reminders for daily habits.**
✓ **Do it at the same time every day.**

When something becomes **part of your routine,** skipping it feels unnatural.

Real-Life Story: The Power of Consistency

Jake wanted to become a top salesperson. But at first, he struggled—he wasn't getting clients, and he felt discouraged.

Instead of giving up, he made a simple rule: **Talk to at least 5 potential clients every day.**

✓ **Some days were easy.**
✓ **Some days were hard.**
✓ **But he never missed a day.**

A year later, he was the highest-earning salesperson in his company.

What made him different? **Not talent. Not luck. Just pure consistency.**

Final Thought: Stay Consistent, Stay Unstoppable

✓ **Success isn't about working hard once—it's about working smart, consistently.**
✓ **Even small efforts, done daily, lead to massive success.**

✓ If you stay consistent, you will win— guaranteed.

You will win—but only if you **keep showing up, every single day.**

Next Chapter: The Courage to Start Over

Now that you know the power of consistency, let's talk about **starting over.** What happens when life knocks you down? How do you rebuild when things don't go as planned? Let's dive into the next chapter.

Chapter 29: The Courage to Start Over

Life doesn't always go as planned.

✓ Businesses fail.
✓ Relationships end.
✓ Goals take longer than expected.
✓ Sometimes, despite your best efforts, things fall apart.

Many people see failure as the end. But winners? **They see it as a chance to start again—smarter, stronger, and better than before.**

Starting over isn't easy. It takes **courage, resilience, and the ability to let go of the past.** But if you master this skill, **nothing will ever stop you.**

Why People Fear Starting Over

Most people resist starting over because they feel:

✗ **Embarrassed.** *"What will people think?"*
✗ **Defeated.** *"I've already failed once. Why try again?"*
✗ **Afraid of repeating mistakes.** *"What if I fail again?"*
✗ **Tired.** *"I don't have the energy to rebuild."*

But here's the truth: **Starting over doesn't mean failure. It means growth.**

✓ Every setback teaches you something valuable.
✓ Every wrong turn helps you find the right path.
✓ Every fresh start is a chance to do things better.

Winners don't let failure define them. They use it to refine them.

How to Start Over (Without Fear or Regret)

1. Accept What Happened—Then Move On

You can't move forward while holding on to the past.

✓ Accept that things didn't go as planned.
✓ Learn the lessons—but don't dwell on the failure.
✓ Forgive yourself and others, then focus on the future.

The faster you let go, **the faster you can rebuild.**

2. Redefine What Success Looks Like Now

Your old plan didn't work. **That's okay.** It's time to create a new one.

✓ Ask yourself: *"What do I really want now?"*
✓ Adjust your goals based on **what you've learned.**
✓ Remember: **Your past does not define your future.**

Sometimes failure pushes you toward **something even better.**

3. Take One Small Step Forward

Starting over can feel overwhelming. The solution? **Focus on one small step at a time.**

✓ If you lost a job → Apply to one new job today.
✓ If a relationship ended → Focus on self-improvement first.
✓ If a business failed → Analyze what went wrong and try again.

You don't have to rebuild overnight—just take the first step.

4. Change the Way You See Failure

Failure is never final unless you quit.

✓ **Albert Einstein** was told he wasn't smart enough.
✓ **Oprah Winfrey** was fired from her first TV job.
✓ **Walt Disney** had multiple businesses fail before building Disney.

The difference? **They started over. And they won.**

If you can shift your mindset, **you'll see failure as a new beginning, not the end.**

5. Build a Stronger Foundation This Time

Instead of rushing back in, **build smarter this time.**

✓ Use your past mistakes to make better decisions.
✓ Focus on consistency, not just quick success.
✓ Surround yourself with people who **support your growth.**

Your second (or third) attempt will be stronger **because you are wiser now.**

Real-Life Story: The Power of Starting Over

Laura spent five years building her dream business—then it failed.

- She felt embarrassed, broke, and defeated.
- She thought about giving up completely.
- She was afraid to start again.

But instead of quitting, she **analyzed what went wrong.**

✓ She realized she needed better financial planning.
✓ She learned how to market her business smarter.
✓ She rebuilt from scratch—this time, with **more experience and confidence.**

Two years later, her new business was thriving. **She didn't let failure stop her—she used it as fuel.**

Final Thought: Starting Over is a Superpower

✓ **Failure isn't the end—it's a lesson.**
✓ **Every setback makes you stronger.**

YOU 'WILL' WIN – THE ONE STOPPING YOU IS 'YOU'

✓ **If you have the courage to start again, you are unstoppable.**

You will win—but only if you **refuse to stay down and start again, no matter what.**

Next Chapter: The Power of Accountability

Now that you know how to start over, let's talk about **accountability.** How do you stay committed to your goals and ensure you follow through? Let's explore in the next chapter.

Chapter 30: The Power of Accountability

It's easy to set goals. It's harder to stick to them.

Most people fail **not because they aren't capable, but because they aren't accountable.**

✓ **They say they'll work out—but no one checks if they do.**
✓ **They promise to start a business—but no one holds them to it.**
✓ **They want success—but they don't have a system to stay on track.**

The truth? **Accountability is the bridge between goals and results.**

If you don't hold yourself accountable—or have someone who does—you will fall into excuses, distractions, and procrastination.

The most successful people don't rely on motivation. They rely on accountability.

Why Accountability is the Key to Success

✓ **It keeps you committed.** You're more likely to follow through when you know someone is watching.
✓ **It eliminates excuses.** You can't justify skipping goals when you have to answer for it.
✓ **It builds self-discipline.** Over time, accountability trains you to stay consistent.

✓ **It helps you push past obstacles.** When you feel like quitting, accountability reminds you to keep going.

The difference between people who **dream** and people who **achieve**? **Accountability.**

Why Most People Lack Accountability

Most people fail at their goals because they:

✗ **Keep their goals to themselves.** No one knows, so no one checks.
✗ **Have no structure to measure progress.** They set goals but don't track them.
✗ **Let themselves off the hook.** They make excuses when things get hard.

If you don't hold yourself accountable, success will always feel out of reach.

How to Build Accountability (And Actually Stick to Your Goals)

1. Announce Your Goals Publicly

✓ **Tell people what you're going to do.**
✓ **Make a commitment that others can see.**
✓ **The fear of looking like a quitter will push you to follow through.**

Example:
✓ Want to get fit? **Post your progress online.**
✓ Want to start a business? **Tell your friends about**

it.
✓ Want to write a book? **Set a public deadline.**

When people know, **you'll feel the pressure to take action.**

2. Get an Accountability Partner

Find someone who will **check in on you**—and call you out if you don't follow through.

✓ **Choose someone who pushes you to be better.**
✓ **Set weekly check-ins to review progress.**
✓ **Make consequences for failing to take action.**

The right accountability partner can double your chances of success.

3. Join a Mastermind or Accountability Group

Winners surround themselves with other winners.

✓ **Being in a group of high achievers keeps you motivated.**
✓ **You'll feel the need to step up when others are progressing.**
✓ **You'll get advice, feedback, and support to stay on track.**

The right group will **elevate your mindset and keep you accountable.**

4. Track Your Progress (Daily & Weekly)

If you don't measure it, you won't improve it.

✓ **Use a habit tracker.** Mark every small win.
✓ **Keep a progress journal.** Write down what's working and what's not.
✓ **Set weekly review sessions.** Reflect on your wins and adjust where needed.

When you track your actions, **you stay in control of your progress.**

5. Set Consequences for Failing

Most people quit because **there's no real cost to failing.**

✓ **Create real consequences** for missing goals.
✓ **Example:** If you don't work out, donate money to a cause you dislike.
✓ **Example:** If you don't complete your task, give $100 to a friend.

When failure has a cost, **you'll push yourself harder to stay on track.**

Real-Life Story: How Accountability Changed Everything

Jake wanted to write a book but kept procrastinating.

Then, he made one change:

✓ He **announced his book publicly** and set a deadline.
✓ He **joined a writers' group** for accountability.
✓ He **hired a coach** to check his progress every week.

Guess what? He finished his book **on time**—all because he had accountability.

The lesson? The right system will push you to succeed—even when motivation fades.

Final Thought: Accountability = Results

✓ If no one is holding you accountable, success will take longer.
✓ If you track your progress, you'll stay consistent.
✓ If you build the right system, you will win— guaranteed.

You will win—but only if you **hold yourself accountable and refuse to quit.**

Next Chapter: Surrounding Yourself with the Right People

Now that you understand accountability, let's talk about **your environment.** How do you find the right people who push you to grow? Let's explore in the next chapter.

Section 4:

Creating Your Path to Success

Chapter 31: Surrounding Yourself with the Right People

You are the average of the **five people you spend the most time with.**

✓ **If you surround yourself with winners, you will rise.**
✗ **If you surround yourself with complainers, you will struggle.**

Your environment shapes your mindset, habits, and success. The fastest way to grow? **Be around people who challenge you, inspire you, and push you to be better.**

If you're serious about winning, **you must carefully choose who you let into your life.**

Why Your Circle Matters

✓ **Your mindset is influenced by those around you.** If you spend time with negative people, you'll absorb their mindset.
✓ **Your standards rise or fall based on your circle.** High achievers push you higher—low achievers pull you down.
✓ **Your energy is affected by who you surround yourself with.** Winners give energy, complainers drain it.

If you want to win, **upgrade your circle.**

The 3 Types of People in Your Life

1☐ **People Who Lift You Up** (Mentors, winners, high achievers)
✓ Inspire you to think bigger
✓ Encourage and support your goals
✓ Challenge you to level up

2☐ **People Who Keep You Stuck** (Average thinkers, excuse-makers)
✓ Complain but never change
✓ Avoid discomfort and challenge
✓ Stay in the same place year after year

3☐ **People Who Drag You Down** (Toxic, negative influences)
✓ Doubt you and discourage your dreams
✓ Bring unnecessary drama into your life
✓ Make excuses for why they can't succeed

If you want success, **spend more time with group #1, limit group #2, and remove group #3.**

How to Surround Yourself with the Right People

1. Find People Who Are Already Winning

✓ Join **masterminds, networking groups, or online communities** with high achievers.
✓ Connect with **mentors or people who have achieved what you want.**
✓ Follow **leaders and successful people** who inspire you.

Success leaves clues. **Learn from those ahead of you.**

2. Cut Out Negative & Toxic Influences

✓ If someone **constantly complains, doubts, or criticizes**, distance yourself.
✓ If someone **always has an excuse but never takes action**, limit your time with them.
✓ If someone **drains your energy instead of fueling your growth**, walk away.

Your energy is valuable. **Don't waste it on people who hold you back.**

3. Spend Time with People Who Challenge You

✓ If you're the smartest person in the room, **you're in the wrong room.**
✓ Surround yourself with people who **push you beyond your limits.**
✓ Be open to **feedback, learning, and growth.**

Growth happens when you're **around people who make you level up.**

4. Become the Kind of Person You Want to Attract

✓ If you want ambitious friends, **be ambitious.**
✓ If you want disciplined people around you, **be disciplined.**
✓ If you want to be around winners, **think, act, and work like one.**

Success attracts success. **Become the person you want in your circle.**

Real-Life Story: How Changing a Circle Changed Everything

Nathan was stuck. His friends were negative, unmotivated, and always made excuses.

One day, he decided to **change his circle.**

✓ He joined a group of entrepreneurs and ambitious thinkers.
✓ He spent time with people who pushed him to take action.
✓ He surrounded himself with winners—and his life transformed.

A year later, Nathan had launched a successful business.

The difference? He stopped spending time with people who held him back.

Final Thought: Your Circle is Your Future

✓ **The people around you shape your success.**
✓ **If you want to win, surround yourself with winners.**
✓ **If you don't like where you are, change your environment.**

You will win—but only if you **build a circle that fuels your growth.**

Next Chapter: Turning Challenges into Opportunities

Now that you know the power of your circle, let's talk about **how to turn struggles into stepping stones.** How do winners transform challenges into success? Let's find out in the next chapter.

Chapter 32: Turning Challenges into Opportunities

Life will throw obstacles in your way. That's guaranteed.

But winners? **They don't just survive challenges—they turn them into opportunities.**

✓ **They use failure as a lesson.**
✓ **They turn setbacks into comebacks.**
✓ **They see obstacles as stepping stones, not roadblocks.**

The difference between success and failure isn't the absence of challenges—it's **how you respond to them.**

If you can master this mindset, **nothing will ever stop you.**

Why Challenges Are Actually Good for You

Most people avoid struggle. But challenges are where **growth happens.**

✓ **Challenges force you to grow.** You develop new skills and resilience.
✓ **Challenges reveal your strengths.** You learn what you're truly capable of.
✓ **Challenges create new opportunities.** Every struggle has the potential to lead to something better.

Instead of fearing obstacles, **start seeing them as opportunities.**

How Winners Turn Challenges into Opportunities

1. Shift from 'Why Me?' to 'What Can I Learn?'

Losers say: *"Why does this always happen to me?"*
Winners say: *"What can I learn from this?"*

✓ **Every failure teaches a lesson.**
✓ **Every setback forces you to improve.**
✓ **Every struggle is shaping you for success.**

If you see challenges as lessons, **you'll never truly fail.**

2. Focus on Solutions, Not Problems

Most people waste time complaining about problems.

Winners? **They focus on solutions.**

✓ Instead of saying *"This is impossible,"* ask *"How can I make this work?"*
✓ Instead of dwelling on failure, analyze *"What can I do differently next time?"*
✓ Instead of waiting for perfect conditions, take action **with what you have.**

The faster you switch to **solution mode,** the faster you'll win.

3. Use Pressure to Your Advantage

✓ Diamonds are formed under pressure.
✓ Muscles grow when they are challenged.
✓ Success comes when you push beyond your comfort zone.

The best things in life happen when you **embrace pressure and rise to the challenge.**

Instead of breaking under stress, **use it as fuel to push harder.**

4. Adapt and Pivot When Needed

Success is about **adjusting, not quitting.**

✓ **If a strategy isn't working, change it.**
✓ **If a door closes, find another way in.**
✓ **If your plan fails, create a better one.**

Winners **don't give up—they adapt.**

Real-Life Story: Turning Failure into Success

Ava lost her job unexpectedly. Instead of feeling defeated, she **saw it as an opportunity.**

✓ She **took online courses** to upgrade her skills.
✓ She **started networking** with high achievers.
✓ She **used the setback as motivation** to launch her own business.

A year later, she was earning more than ever—**all because she turned a challenge into an opportunity.**

Final Thought: Challenges Make You Stronger

✓ **Every obstacle is a chance to grow.**
✓ **Every failure is a lesson, not the end.**
✓ **Every struggle prepares you for something greater.**

You will win—but only if you **see challenges as stepping stones, not stop signs.**

Next Chapter: Why Passion Alone Is Not Enough

Now that you know how to turn challenges into opportunities, let's talk about **why passion isn't enough for success.** What else do you need to make your dreams a reality? Let's find out in the next chapter.

Chapter 33: Why Passion Alone Is Not Enough

"Follow your passion, and success will follow."

Sounds great, right?

But here's the truth: **Passion alone is not enough.**

✓ **Passion gives you excitement, but not results.**
✓ **Passion makes you start, but discipline makes you finish.**
✓ **Passion without skill, strategy, and consistency leads nowhere.**

If passion were enough, the world would be full of successful musicians, writers, and entrepreneurs.

But success requires **more than just love for something—it requires action, learning, and persistence.**

Why Passion Alone Fails

✕ Passion Fades Over Time
The excitement you feel at the beginning **won't always last.**

✓ What happens when you no longer "feel like" working?
✓ What happens when passion turns into hard work?
✓ What happens when you hit obstacles?

Passion alone won't push you through tough days—**discipline and commitment will.**

✘ Passion Doesn't Equal Skill

You can love something, but that doesn't mean you're good at it—**yet.**

✓ Many people are passionate about music but never practice enough to master it.
✓ Many people are passionate about writing but never develop storytelling skills.
✓ Many people are passionate about starting a business but never learn how to run one.

If you want to succeed, **you must develop skills that turn passion into results.**

✘ Passion Without a Plan = No Progress

Many passionate people fail because **they have no strategy.**

✓ They rely on excitement instead of discipline.
✓ They don't track their progress or adjust their approach.
✓ They chase ideas without a clear direction.

Success isn't just about feeling inspired—it's about **taking consistent, smart action.**

What You Need Besides Passion

1. Skill Development

Passion is the spark, but **skills are the fuel.**

✓ If you love music, **practice and study it seriously.**
✓ If you love writing, **master storytelling and editing.**
✓ If you love business, **learn sales, marketing, and finance.**

The more skilled you become, **the more valuable your passion becomes.**

2. Self-Discipline

✗ Passion makes you excited **on good days.**
✓ Discipline makes you show up **even on bad days.**

✓ Winners don't wait for motivation—they stick to their routine.
✓ They don't rely on passion—they rely on **consistent action.**
✓ They don't quit when things get hard—they **push through.**

If you master discipline, **you can succeed in anything.**

3. Strategy and Execution

A dream without a plan is just a wish.

✓ Set **clear goals.**
✓ Create **a step-by-step plan.**
✓ Track **your progress and adjust when needed.**

Success comes from **smart action, not just excitement.**

4. The Ability to Adapt

Passion can blind you.

✓ If something isn't working, **be willing to adjust.**
✓ If your industry changes, **learn new skills.**
✓ If one path fails, **find another.**

The most successful people **pivot when necessary.**

Real-Life Story: How Passion + Strategy Created Success

Daniel loved photography. But for years, it was just a hobby.

Then he realized: **Passion wasn't enough—he needed a strategy.**

✓ He **studied photography professionally.**
✓ He **built an online portfolio and learned marketing.**
✓ He **treated it like a business, not just a passion.**

Today, Daniel runs a thriving photography business.

His passion didn't make him successful—**his skills, discipline, and strategy did.**

Final Thought: Passion + Action = Success

✓ **Passion is the starting point—but not the finish line.**
✓ **Passion without discipline leads nowhere.**
✓ **If you combine passion with skill, strategy, and consistency—you will win.**

You will win—but only if you **turn passion into disciplined action.**

Next Chapter: How to Keep Going When You Feel Like Giving Up

Now that you know passion isn't enough, let's talk about **what to do when you hit tough times.** How do you keep pushing forward when success feels far away? Let's find out in the next chapter.

Chapter 34: How to Keep Going When You Feel Like Giving Up

Every winner has felt like quitting at some point.

✓ They faced rejection.
✓ They doubted themselves.
✓ They struggled to see progress.

But the difference between winners and everyone else? **They kept going.**

Success isn't about never feeling tired, frustrated, or discouraged. It's about **pushing forward anyway.**

If you're struggling, doubting, or thinking about quitting—this chapter is for you.

Why People Give Up Too Soon

Most people quit **not because they can't succeed, but because they give up too early.**

✗ **They expect quick results.** When success takes longer than expected, they lose patience.
✗ **They let failure discourage them.** Instead of learning from mistakes, they stop trying.
✗ **They compare themselves to others.** They feel behind and assume they'll never make it.
✗ **They lose motivation.** They wait to "feel" inspired instead of building discipline.

The truth? **If you quit, you guarantee failure. If you keep going, success is still possible.**

How to Keep Going When You Want to Quit

1. Focus on Why You Started

When things get tough, **remind yourself why you started in the first place.**

✓ What was your goal?
✓ What excited you about this journey?
✓ What happens if you quit now?

Going back to your "why" **reignites your motivation.**

2. Take One Small Step Forward

Feeling stuck? Overwhelmed? **Just take one small action.**

✓ Write one sentence.
✓ Make one phone call.
✓ Do five minutes of work.

Progress—even tiny progress—**creates momentum.**

3. Stop Expecting Fast Results

✗ Success doesn't happen overnight.
✗ Mastery takes years, not weeks.
✗ Every great achiever struggled before they won.

The best things in life **take time. Be patient. Keep moving.**

4. Learn From Failure—Don't Run From It

Every failure is **a lesson, not a reason to quit.**

✓ If something didn't work, analyze why.
✓ Adjust your approach instead of stopping.
✓ Use failure as feedback to improve.

Every setback **is setting you up for a comeback.**

5. Take Breaks, But Don't Quit

✓ Rest when needed, but **don't walk away forever.**
✓ Step back, recharge, and come back stronger.
✓ Winners know **when to pause—but they never quit.**

It's okay to feel tired—**but don't let exhaustion turn into giving up.**

Real-Life Story: Pushing Through Instead of Quitting

Emily started a business, but after a year, she had no big results.

She felt like quitting. **She thought maybe she wasn't meant for success.**

But instead of giving up:

✓ She adjusted her marketing strategy.
✓ She kept learning and improving.
✓ She reminded herself of **why she started.**

A year later, her business was thriving.

She didn't win because she was lucky—she won because she refused to quit.

Final Thought: Winners Keep Going

✓ **Everyone struggles—but not everyone quits.**
✓ **The only way to truly fail is to stop trying.**
✓ **If you keep going, success will come.**

You will win—but only if you **push through when it gets tough.**

Next Chapter: The Role of Gratitude in Success

Now that you know how to keep going, let's talk about **the power of gratitude.** How does appreciating what you have help you achieve even more? Let's explore in the next chapter.

Chapter 35: The Role of Gratitude in Success

Most people chase success, thinking **"I'll be happy when I achieve my goals."**

But here's the truth: **Gratitude creates success—not the other way around.**

✓ **People who appreciate what they have attract more opportunities.**
✓ **People who focus on abundance, not lack, stay motivated.**
✓ **People who celebrate small wins build the momentum for bigger victories.**

The secret to achieving more? **Be grateful for what you already have.**

Why Gratitude is a Superpower

Gratitude isn't just about feeling good—it actually helps you win.

✓ **Gratitude shifts your mindset.** Instead of focusing on what's missing, you focus on possibilities.
✓ **Gratitude reduces stress.** A positive mind handles challenges better.
✓ **Gratitude boosts resilience.** It reminds you of how far you've come.

When you appreciate the journey, success becomes easier.

How Lack of Gratitude Holds You Back

✘ **You feel like nothing is ever enough.** No matter what you achieve, you keep chasing more.
✘ **You get discouraged easily.** Instead of celebrating progress, you focus on what's missing.
✘ **You compare yourself to others.** Instead of seeing your growth, you only see what others have.

Winners know that **happiness and success come from appreciating the process—not just the outcome.**

How to Use Gratitude to Fuel Your Success

1. Start Each Day with Gratitude

✓ Write down **three things** you're grateful for each morning.
✓ Focus on **progress, not perfection.**
✓ Gratitude shifts your mind to **abundance, not lack.**

The more you appreciate what you have, **the more you attract success.**

2. Celebrate Small Wins

Success isn't just about big achievements—it's about **daily progress.**

✓ Got through a tough day? **That's a win.**
✓ Took one small step toward your goal? **That's a win.**
✓ Learned something new? **That's a win.**

The more you acknowledge progress, **the easier it is to stay motivated.**

3. Focus on What's Working (Not What's Missing)

Most people focus on **what they lack.** Winners focus on **what they have.**

✓ Instead of saying *"I don't have enough success,"* say *"I have the skills to create success."*
✓ Instead of saying *"I'm not where I want to be,"* say *"I'm further than I was before."*

Your mindset shapes your reality. Focus on the positives, and success will follow.

4. Express Gratitude to Others

✓ Thank people who support you.
✓ Appreciate small acts of kindness.
✓ Acknowledge the value others bring into your life.

Success isn't just about what you achieve—it's about **who you become along the way.**

Real-Life Story: How Gratitude Changed Everything

Ethan used to focus only on what he didn't have.

✓ He constantly compared himself to others.
✓ He felt like he was never making enough progress.
✓ He was always chasing the next thing, never satisfied.

Then he started practicing gratitude.

✓ He focused on his daily progress.
✓ He celebrated small wins.
✓ He reminded himself how far he had come.

Soon, he was **happier, more focused, and more successful.**

His success didn't change his gratitude—**his gratitude changed his success.**

Final Thought: Gratitude is the Key to Winning

✓ **Gratitude makes success feel easier.**
✓ **When you appreciate what you have, you create more opportunities.**
✓ **Happiness isn't something you get after success—it's something that helps you create it.**

You will win—but only if you **stay grateful while chasing your goals.**

Next Chapter: The Importance of Self-Reflection

Now that you understand gratitude, let's talk about **self-reflection.** How do you analyze your progress, make better decisions, and stay on the right path? Let's explore in the next chapter.

Chapter 36: The Importance of Self-Reflection

Success isn't just about action—it's about **learning from your journey.**

✓ **Winners don't just move forward blindly.** They stop, reflect, and adjust.
✓ **They learn from past mistakes.**
✓ **They recognize what's working and what's not.**
✓ **They stay aware of their progress and mindset.**

Self-reflection is like a **compass for success.** If you don't check your direction, **you might be running fast—but in the wrong way.**

Why Self-Reflection is Essential for Growth

✓ **It helps you see your progress.** Most people are improving but don't realize it.
✓ **It helps you fix mistakes faster.** If something isn't working, reflection helps you adjust.
✓ **It strengthens self-awareness.** You understand yourself better and make smarter choices.
✓ **It builds confidence.** When you reflect on how far you've come, you realize how much you've grown.

Winners don't just work hard. They work smart— and self-reflection is how they do it.

Why Most People Avoid Self-Reflection

✗ **They're afraid to face their mistakes.**
✗ **They're too busy moving forward to stop and look back.**
✗ **They assume they'll naturally improve without evaluating themselves.**

But here's the truth: **If you don't reflect, you repeat the same mistakes.**

Success isn't just about effort—it's about **learning, adjusting, and growing.**

How to Practice Powerful Self-Reflection

1. Ask Yourself the Right Questions

Take time every week to reflect. Ask:

✓ **What went well this week?**
✓ **What could I have done better?**
✓ **What lessons did I learn?**
✓ **What actions can I take to improve?**

The answers will **guide your next moves.**

2. Keep a Success & Growth Journal

✓ Write down your wins—big or small.
✓ Record the lessons from your failures.
✓ Track your goals, habits, and mindset shifts.

When you write things down, you see your growth clearly.

3. Learn from Your Failures—Not Just Your Wins

Most people only celebrate success. But winners **analyze failures just as much.**

✓ **What caused the failure?**
✓ **What can I change next time?**
✓ **How can I turn this into a lesson instead of a setback?**

Mistakes aren't failures **if you learn from them.**

4. Set a Weekly Reflection Routine

✓ **Every Sunday, review your past week.**
✓ **Look at your goals and see if you're on track.**
✓ **Adjust your plan based on what's working and what's not.**

Self-reflection is most powerful **when done regularly.**

Real-Life Story: How Self-Reflection Led to a Breakthrough

James was working hard but felt stuck.

✓ He was putting in the hours, but progress felt slow.
✓ He kept repeating the same mistakes.
✓ He wasn't sure what was holding him back.

Then he started reflecting weekly.

✓ He realized he was spending too much time on low-impact tasks.
✓ He noticed he wasn't taking enough risks.
✓ He adjusted his strategy—and his results skyrocketed.

His breakthrough didn't come from working harder—**it came from reflecting smarter.**

Final Thought: Reflection Creates Acceleration

✓ Success isn't just about moving—it's about moving in the right direction.
✓ If you don't reflect, you'll keep repeating mistakes.
✓ The best way to grow faster is to learn from every experience.

You will win—but only if you **take time to reflect, learn, and adjust.**

Next Chapter: Avoiding Burnout While Chasing Your Dreams

Now that you understand self-reflection, let's talk about **how to stay energized.** Success is great—but how do you make sure you don't burn out along the way? Let's find out in the next chapter.

Chapter 37: Avoiding Burnout While Chasing Your Dreams

Success requires hard work, discipline, and consistency.

But what happens when **you push too hard, too fast, for too long?**

Burnout.

✓ **You feel exhausted—mentally, physically, emotionally.**
✓ **You lose motivation, even for things you once loved.**
✓ **You start questioning if it's all worth it.**

Burnout doesn't just slow you down—it can **completely derail your journey.**

That's why winners don't just work hard. **They know how to sustain energy, balance effort, and keep going without breaking down.**

Why Burnout Happens

✗ **You ignore rest.** You think taking breaks means you're falling behind.
✗ **You overload yourself.** You try to do everything at once.
✗ **You never disconnect.** Your mind is constantly in "work mode."
✗ **You push through exhaustion instead of listening to your body.**

If you don't manage your energy, **your body will force you to stop.**

The key? **Work hard, but work smart.**

How to Avoid Burnout While Still Winning

1. Schedule Rest Like You Schedule Work

Most people plan work but forget to plan **recovery.**

✓ **Take one full day off every week.**
✓ **Set daily 'no-work' hours.** (For example, no work after 8 PM.)
✓ **Take short breaks every few hours.**

Your brain needs time to recharge **so you can perform at your best.**

2. Set Clear Boundaries

Burnout happens when you **never turn off.**

✓ **If you work from home, have a dedicated 'work' space.**
✓ **Avoid checking emails late at night.**
✓ **Learn to say NO to tasks that drain you.**

Success is about **sustainability, not just speed.**

3. Prioritize Sleep and Health

✗ You can't perform at your best if you're always tired.
✗ Poor sleep = Low energy, bad decisions, and lack of motivation.

✓ **Aim for 7–8 hours of quality sleep.**
✓ **Fuel your body with the right food.**
✓ **Move daily—exercise is a stress reliever, not just a fitness goal.**

Winners don't sacrifice health for success—they know **health is the foundation of success.**

4. Focus on High-Impact Work, Not Just Busy Work

Burnout isn't just about working too much—it's about working on **the wrong things.**

✓ **Prioritize tasks that truly move you forward.**
✓ **Cut out distractions and low-value activities.**
✓ **Use the 80/20 Rule—80% of results come from 20% of efforts.**

Work smarter, not just harder.

5. Celebrate Progress (Even Small Wins)

✗ If you only focus on the big goal, you'll always feel behind.
✓ But if you celebrate small progress, you'll stay motivated.

✓ **Finished an important task? Acknowledge it.**
✓ **Hit a small milestone? Reward yourself.**
✓ **Made it through a tough day? That's a win, too.**

Success is a journey. **Enjoy the process, not just the destination.**

Real-Life Story: How a Burned-Out Entrepreneur Recovered

Liam was building his business **but working 16-hour days.**

✓ He skipped meals.
✓ He barely slept.
✓ He had no personal life.

Then, burnout hit. **He lost motivation, got sick, and almost gave up.**

He made one change: **He started prioritizing rest, boundaries, and smart work.**

✓ He worked **fewer hours but focused only on high-impact tasks.**
✓ He **scheduled rest and personal time like business meetings.**
✓ He **started exercising and sleeping better.**

Within months, he was **more productive, healthier, and more successful than ever.**

His secret? He stopped chasing success recklessly and started managing his energy wisely.

Final Thought: Success is a Marathon, Not a Sprint

✓ **Burnout is preventable—but only if you manage your energy wisely.**
✓ **Work hard, but make sure you can sustain it for the long run.**
✓ **If you want to win, take care of yourself— because YOU are your greatest asset.**

You will win—but only if you **protect your energy while chasing your dreams.**

Next Chapter: The Art of Saying No

Now that you understand how to avoid burnout, let's talk about **one of the most powerful skills for success— saying no.** How do you protect your time, energy, and focus? Let's find out in the next chapter.

Chapter 38: The Art of Saying No

One of the biggest reasons people fail is **saying "yes" too often.**

✓ They take on too many responsibilities.
✓ They agree to things they don't want to do.
✓ They get distracted by other people's priorities instead of focusing on their own.

But winners? **They protect their time, energy, and focus.**

They understand that every time they say **"yes" to something unimportant, they are saying "no" to something that truly matters.**

If you want to win, you must master the art of saying NO.

Why Most People Struggle to Say No

✗ **Fear of disappointing others** – They don't want to upset people.
✗ **Fear of missing out (FOMO)** – They think every opportunity is important.
✗ **Trying to be nice** – They believe saying no makes them selfish.
✗ **Lack of clear priorities** – They don't know what truly matters.

But here's the truth: **Every successful person knows how to say no.**

✓ **Warren Buffett** once said: *"The difference between successful people and very successful people is that very successful people say no to almost everything."*

How Saying No Leads to More Success

✓ **It protects your time.** You stay focused on what truly matters.
✓ **It reduces stress.** You avoid unnecessary commitments.
✓ **It increases your energy.** You say yes only to things that align with your goals.
✓ **It helps you build boundaries.** People respect you more when they know you have limits.

If you struggle with **overcommitment, distractions, or feeling overwhelmed,** learning to say no will change your life.

How to Say No Without Feeling Guilty

1. Get Clear on Your Priorities

If you don't know what matters most, **you'll say yes to everything.**

✓ **Decide what's truly important in your life.**
✓ **Write down your top 3 priorities.**
✓ **Before saying yes to anything, ask: "Does this align with my priorities?"**

If it doesn't, **say no without guilt.**

2. Say No With Confidence

✘ Weak response: *"Umm... I'm not sure... maybe..."*
✓ Strong response: *"I appreciate the offer, but I can't commit to this right now."*

Be direct. Be clear. Be firm.

You don't need a long explanation—**just a confident "no" is enough.**

3. Offer an Alternative (If Needed)

If you don't want to sound harsh, you can soften your "no" by offering an alternative.

✓ *"I can't do this, but I can help in a smaller way."*
✓ *"I don't have time now, but I can check back later."*

This way, you **maintain good relationships while still protecting your time.**

4. Use the "Delayed No" Strategy

If you feel pressured, don't give an immediate answer.

✓ Say: *"Let me think about it and get back to you."*
✓ This gives you time to decide **without feeling forced.**

Most of the time, **you'll realize you don't want to do it—and saying no becomes easier.**

5. Remember: Every Yes is a No to Something Else

✓ Saying yes to too many meetings? **You're saying no to focused work.**
✓ Saying yes to toxic relationships? **You're saying no to mental peace.**
✓ Saying yes to every social event? **You're saying no to personal growth time.**

If you want to win, **your time and energy must be spent on what truly matters.**

Real-Life Story: How Saying No Changed Everything

Ryan was a **people-pleaser.**

✓ He said yes to every invitation.
✓ He took on extra work he didn't want to do.
✓ He never had time for his own goals.

Then he started **saying no.**

✓ He turned down unnecessary meetings.
✓ He stopped overcommitting to things that drained him.
✓ He focused on his priorities.

Soon, **his productivity skyrocketed.** His relationships improved. His stress disappeared.

Saying no gave him back control over his life.

Final Thought: Saying No is Saying Yes to Yourself

✓ **You don't have to do everything.**
✓ **You don't have to please everyone.**
✓ **Your time is valuable—spend it wisely.**

You will win—but only if you **learn to say no to distractions and yes to what truly matters.**

Next Chapter: Your Success Formula – Defining What Winning Means to You

Now that you've learned to say no, let's talk about **your personal definition of success.** What does winning look like for YOU? Let's explore in the next chapter.

Chapter 39: Your Success Formula – Defining What Winning Means to You

What does success mean to you?

For some, it's **financial freedom.**
For others, it's **happiness and peace of mind.**
For some, it's **impact and legacy.**

There is no single definition of success. What matters is **how YOU define it.**

If you don't know what success means to you, you'll:
✗ Chase other people's goals instead of your own.
✗ Feel empty even after achieving things.
✗ Never know when you've "won."

Winning is personal. It's time to define your own success formula.

Why Defining Your Own Success is Important

✓ It keeps you focused. You stop chasing things that don't truly matter to you.
✓ It gives you direction. You know exactly what you're working toward.
✓ It makes success fulfilling. You don't just achieve—you achieve what matters to YOU.

If you don't define success for yourself, society will do it for you.

How to Define Your Own Success Formula

1. Ask Yourself: What Does Success Look Like for Me?

Forget what the world says. Forget what others expect.

Ask yourself:
✓ What makes me feel truly fulfilled?
✓ What do I want my life to look like in 5, 10, 20 years?
✓ What kind of impact do I want to make?

Your answers will reveal **what truly matters to you.**

2. Identify Your Core Values

Success is meaningless if it's not aligned with your values.

✓ If freedom matters most to you, success isn't a corporate job—it's building something of your own.
✓ If family is your top priority, success isn't working 80-hour weeks—it's having time with loved ones.
✓ If creativity drives you, success isn't just money—it's being able to express yourself.

When your success aligns with your values, it feels right.

3. Define the Key Areas of Your Life That Matter Most

Success isn't just about money or career—it's about **balance in all areas of life.**

Define what success looks like in these key areas:
✓ **Health** – What does being healthy mean for you?
✓ **Wealth** – How much financial freedom do you want?
✓ **Relationships** – What kind of friendships and family life do you want?
✓ **Growth** – How do you want to keep learning and evolving?
✓ **Impact** – How do you want to contribute to the world?

Your version of success should include ALL areas of your life.

4. Set Your Own Success Metrics

Most people measure success **by comparing themselves to others.**

✗ **Wrong approach:** *"I'll be successful when I have more than others."*
✓ **Right approach:** *"I'll be successful when I reach my personal goals."*

Set your own metrics for success.
✓ "I will consider myself successful when I can travel without worrying about money."
✓ "I will feel successful when I build a career that aligns with my passion."

✓ "I will know I've won when I wake up every day excited about life."

Your success = **Your rules.**

5. Accept That Success Will Evolve Over Time

✓ What success means to you today **might change in five years.**
✓ That's okay—**growth brings new perspectives.**
✓ Stay open to **redefining your goals as you evolve.**

The key is to **keep checking in with yourself** so you always know you're on the right path.

Real-Life Story: Finding a Personal Success Formula

Ethan chased society's version of success—high-paying job, luxury lifestyle.

✓ He made money, but he felt empty.
✓ He was successful by others' standards, but not by his own.
✓ One day, he asked: *"What do I truly want?"*

He realized:
✓ He valued **freedom more than money.**
✓ He wanted **to travel and work on his own terms.**
✓ He redefined success as **having control over his time.**

Today, he's happier than ever—**because he follows HIS success formula, not someone else's.**

Final Thought: Success is Personal

✓ **Your success should align with your values and dreams.**
✓ **Don't chase someone else's definition of success—create your own.**
✓ **When you define success for yourself, you'll know when you've truly won.**

You will win—but only if you **chase the right victory for YOU.**

Next Chapter: You Will Win – Writing Your Own Success Story

Now that you've defined success, it's time to **take ownership of your journey.** How do you write your own success story, one chapter at a time? Let's explore in the final chapter.

Chapter 40: You Will Win – Writing Your Own Success Story

You've made it to the final chapter.

By now, you understand that success isn't about luck, talent, or waiting for the perfect moment.

Success is a choice. Winning is a decision.

✓ You know what holds you back—and how to overcome it.
✓ You know how to rewire your mindset for success.
✓ You know how to take action and stay consistent.
✓ You know how to define success on your own terms.

Now, the only thing left to do is **write your own success story.**

Because no one else is coming to do it for you.

Your Life is a Book – You Decide the Story

Right now, you're in the middle of your story.

✗ Maybe you've struggled.
✗ Maybe you've failed before.
✗ Maybe you've doubted yourself.

But guess what? **The past doesn't define the ending.**

✓ **Every great success story has obstacles.**
✓ **Every winner has faced challenges.**
✓ **Every champion has wanted to quit—but didn't.**

Your story is still being written. **And you hold the pen.**

How to Take Control and Win

1. Stop Waiting – Start Moving

There is never a perfect time. There is only **now.**

✓ **Stop overthinking.**
✓ **Stop waiting for motivation.**
✓ **Stop letting fear hold you back.**

Just take the first step. Then another. Then another. **That's how winning happens.**

2. Own Your Journey – No More Excuses

✗ No blaming circumstances.
✗ No blaming others.
✗ No blaming the past.

✓ **You are responsible for your own success.**
✓ **No one else is coming to save you—it's on YOU.**
✓ **Take full ownership, and you take full control.**

3. Be the Hero, Not the Victim

Every great story has a hero. And every hero faces struggles.

✓ **Will you rise above your challenges or let them define you?**
✓ **Will you push forward, even when it's hard?**
✓ **Will you turn pain into power and obstacles into opportunities?**

Heroes fight through setbacks. **Be the hero of your own story.**

4. Keep Writing – Keep Going

✓ If today wasn't great, **tomorrow is a new page.**
✓ If you fail, **you get to rewrite your approach.**
✓ If you feel lost, **you can always reset and refocus.**

No matter where you are now, **your story isn't over.**

Keep writing. Keep building. Keep winning.

Real-Life Story: The Power of Deciding to Win

Mia struggled for years.

✓ She had big dreams but never took action.
✓ She let fear and doubt hold her back.
✓ She kept waiting for the "right time."

One day, she realized: **The right time is NOW.**

✓ She took ownership of her life.
✓ She stopped making excuses and started taking action.
✓ She stayed consistent—**even when progress was slow.**

A year later, she was living the life she once only dreamed about.

Her success didn't happen overnight. **It happened the moment she decided to win.**

Final Thought: You Will Win – If You Choose To

✓ **You have the knowledge.**
✓ **You have the tools.**
✓ **Now, you must take action.**

No more waiting. No more excuses. **Your success story starts now.**

So go write it. And make it legendary.

Thank You for Reading

This book is just the beginning. Your journey is yours to create.

Now, take what you've learned—and go win.

Because the only thing stopping you... is you.

Printed in Great Britain
by Amazon